K

EARLY DETECTION AND COGNITIVE THERAPY FOR PEOPLE AT HIGH RISK OF DEVELOPING PSYCHOSIS

EARLY DETECTION AND COGNITIVE THERAPY FOR PEOPLE AT HIGH RISK OF DEVELOPING PSYCHOSIS

A TREATMENT APPROACH

Paul French
*Department of Psychology, Bolton, Salford &
Trafford Mental Health Trust*

Anthony P. Morrison
*Department of Psychology, Bolton, Salford &
Trafford Mental Health Trust and
Department of Psychology, University of Manchester*

John Wiley & Sons, Ltd

Other Wiley Editorial Offices

John Wiley & Sons Inc., 111 River Street, Hoboken, NJ 07030, USA

Jossey-Bass, 989 Market Street, San Francisco, CA 94103-1741, USA

Wiley-VCH Verlag GmbH, Boschstr. 12, D-69469 Weinheim, Germany

John Wiley & Sons Australia Ltd, 33 Park Road, Milton, Queensland 4064, Australia

John Wiley & Sons (Asia) Pte Ltd, 2 Clementi Loop #02-01, Jin Xing Distripark, Singapore 129809

John Wiley & Sons Canada Ltd, 22 Worcester Road, Etobicoke, Ontario, Canada M9W 1L1

Wiley also publishes its books in a variety of electronic formats. Some content that appears in print may not be available
in electronic books.

Library of Congress Cataloging-in-Publication Data

French, Paul, 1963–
Early detection and cognitive therapy for people at high risk of
developing psychosis : a treatment approach / Paul French, Anthony P. Morrison.
        p.   cm.
     Includes bibliographical references and index.
     ISBN 0-470-86314-5 (cloth : alk. paper) – ISBN 0-470-86315-3 (pbk. : alk. paper)
     1. Psychoses–Prevention.   2. Psychoses–Diagnosis.   3. Psychoses–Treatment.
4. Cognitive therapy.   I. Morrison, Anthony P., 1969–   II. Title.
RC512 .F7197   2004
616.89′05–dc22   2003020689

British Library Cataloguing in Publication Data

A catalogue record for this book is available from the British Library

ISBN 0-470-86314-5 (hbk)
ISBN 0-470-86315-3 (pbk)

Typeset in 10/12pt Times and Helvetica by TechBooks Electronic Services, New Delhi, India
Printed and bound in Great Britain by TJ International Ltd, Padstow, Cornwall
This book is printed on acid-free paper responsibly manufactured from sustainable forestry
in which at least two trees are planted for each one used for paper production.

CONTENTS

List of Figures and Appendices   vii

About the Authors   ix

Foreword by Max Birchwood   xi

Introduction   xiii

Acknowledgements   xvii

Part I: BACKGROUND   **1**

1 The Importance of Early Recognition   3

2 How to Identify At-Risk Groups   9

3 Which Prevention Strategy to Adopt   23

Part II: COGNITIVE THERAPY FOR PREVENTION OF PSYCHOSIS   **27**

4 Why Cognitive Therapy?   29

5 Engagement   37

6 Theory, Assessment and Formulation   45

Part III: CHANGE STRATEGIES   **55**

7 Normalisation   57

8 Generating and Evaluating Alternative Explanations   65

9 Safety Behaviours   75

10 Metacognitive Beliefs   87

11 'I Am Different' and Other Core Beliefs   93

12 Social Isolation   101

13 Relapse Prevention   111

14 Conclusions   117

Appendices   121

References   135

Index   143

LIST OF FIGURES AND APPENDICES

Figures

1.1 Duration of untreated psychosis and duration of untreated illness   4

2.1 Graph demonstrating age of onset for schizophrenia   12

2.2 Table demonstrating PANSS criteria for defining at-risk groups   16

2.3 Potential referral sources   17

2.4 Primary care guidelines for identification of suspected or first-episode psychosis   18

2.5 Graph demonstrating referrals and suitability   20

4.1 Experiment sheet   35

5.1 Formulation indicating event, belief about event, feelings and behaviours   40

6.1 Morrison's model of psychosis   46

6.2 Client-friendly version of Morrison's model of psychosis   52

6.3 Idiosyncratic version of Morrison's model of psychosis   53

8.1 Explanations for experiences form   70

8.2 Idiosyncratic formulation indicating the importance of interpretation of intrusions in a catastrophic manner   71

8.3 Idiosyncratic formulation indicating the importance of interpretation of intrusions using normalising information   72

8.4 Example of evidence for and against a belief   73

9.1 Examples of safety behaviours   76

9.2   Form for generating alternatives   83

11.1 Idiosyncratic case formulation   97

12.1 French et al.'s model of early psychotic symptoms   102

12.2 Problem list   107

12.3 Idiosyncratic version of French et al.'s model   108

Appendices   121

1 Client-friendly formulation   123

2 Form for generating alternatives   125

3 Experiment sheet   127

4 Weekly activity sheet   129

5 Client-treatment rationale – BLIPS group rationale   130

6 Client-treatment rationale – attenuated symptoms group rationale   131

7 Client-treatment rationale – family group rationale   132

8 Primary care guidelines for identification of suspected or
   first-episode psychosis   133

ABOUT THE AUTHORS

Paul French is co-ordinator of a specialist clinical team based at Bolton, Salford & Trafford Mental Health Trust offering cognitive interventions for people who are considered at high risk of developing psychosis. He has worked in mental health since 1989 and has always been interested in the provision of services for people with psychosis having worked in a variety of inpatient and community settings. More recently, he has developed a research interest in working with people at high risk of developing psychosis. He has published a number of articles relating to early psychosis and particularly the provision of psychological interventions in early psychosis.

Anthony P. Morrison is a reader in psychology at the University of Manchester and is also programme co-ordinator for a specialist programme of care for people with early psychosis in Bolton, Salford & Trafford Mental Health Trust. He has published a number of articles on cognitive therapy for psychosis and experimental studies of cognitive processes in psychosis. He has been involved in a number of treatment trials for cognitive therapy for psychosis and has a special interest in the cognitive theory of and therapy for hearing voices. More recently, he has developed a research interest in working with people at high risk of developing psychosis and the links between trauma and psychosis. He was awarded the May Davidson Award 2002 for his contributions to clinical psychology.

FOREWORD

For too long, services to people with psychosis have been crippled by the dead hand of the Kraepelinian 'dementia model' of psychosis. Even in these enlightened times in mental health care, containment-oriented care pervades our services. Thus, in contrast with every other area of health care, the language of prevention has barely registered in psychiatry. Recent years have, at last, witnessed a sea change in our thinking and the concept of 'early intervention' in psychosis has forced its way on to the scientific and services agenda.

The possibility of detecting and treating emerging psychosis is at the core of this new approach, ignited by the pioneering work of Alison Yung and Patrick McGorry in Melbourne. This paradigm is informed by the concept of 'indicated prevention', in which a group of individuals has been identified, by virtue of the presence of low-level or precursor psychotic symptoms, to be at high risk of transition to psychosis. Neuroleptic medication has been the mainstay of early treatment in the research hitherto. Concerns have been raised, however, about the ethics of drug treatment at such an early stage and whether service users find it acceptable. Available evidence suggests that service users are reluctant to consent to treatment trials involving medication and, if they do so, tend to drop out early. What has been badly needed is an effective and acceptable *verbal*-based therapeutic strategy to provide treatment options for the researcher and clinician.

French and Morrison have developed just such an approach. In this book, they present their cognitive treatment model in a very engaging and lucid way, making maximum use of clinical material and case examples. What I particularly like about their approach is that the therapeutic focus is not solely on emerging psychotic thinking, but is formulation driven, based on an agenda set by the client him/herself, which usually embraces problems of social interaction and social cognition. What is also clear from reading this book is that the clients they treat are *already* help-seeking but their ambiguous presentation leads to an inconsistent and *ad hoc* response from services because of the absence of a treatment protocol. French and Morrison's theoretical framework is coherent and well articulated and brings to bear cognitive and interpersonal factors that we know to be active in established psychosis. The therapy they describe has been validated in a well-controlled randomised trial showing that psychosis can be prevented, or at least delayed, in a substantial majority of those at risk of transition to psychosis.

Paul French and Tony Morrison deserve our congratulations and thanks for moving back this important frontier, which only a few years ago would have been regarded as an impossible dream.

Max Birchwood

Professor of Clinical Psychology, University of Birmingham, and Director of Early Intervention Services; Director of Research and Development at the Northern Birmingham Mental Health Trust
September, 2003

INTRODUCTION

There has been a great deal of concern regarding the validity of the diagnosis of schizophrenia (Bentall, 1990) and this concern is magnified in the early course of the development of psychosis. The utility of the diagnosis is also questionable in terms of treatment, and a symptom-based approach appears to be more suitable. It has been suggested that the concept of schizophrenia is not particularly useful when considering people at risk of developing psychosis. Significantly, many people at risk of developing psychosis are concerned with the onset of 'madness' and, unfortunately, the diagnosis of schizophrenia is perceived as encapsulating the essence of what the term 'madness' entails. Clearly, this is neither accurate nor helpful, although the label is frequently viewed in this way and the media often serve to enhance this notion. An alternative approach is to utilise the broader concept of psychosis, and this is the approach that has been adopted by many groups who are working with people in the early phase of psychotic disorders. Therefore, in this book we will use the term 'psychosis' in preference to terms such as schizophrenia. We recognise that, for some people, 'psychosis' can be as stigmatising and pathologising a label as 'schizophrenia'. However, we adopt the term as a short hand for unusual perceptual experiences and beliefs, and do not assume that such phenomena are abnormal or pathological. On the contrary, as illustrated in Chapter 7, we view such experiences as part of the continuum of normal experience, and we assume it is the interpretation or appraisal of such phenomena that causes any distress or disability. Therefore, we are not trying to prevent people from experiencing unusual beliefs or perceptual phenomena, as we recognise that they can be functional and important in people's lives. Rather, we are trying to help people to reduce distress and disability, should they choose to do so.

The treatment we describe is a psychological treatment, cognitive therapy (CT), and in this book we outline the specific strategies we have developed for working with a client group who are at risk of developing psychosis. The treatment is heavily influenced by the literature on anxiety disorders, as many of the processes involved in the development and maintenance of distress resulting from psychotic experiences are similar to those present in anxiety disorders (for example, misinterpretations, preoccupation with threat, selective attention and metacognition).

There is now a long history of psychological interventions for psychotic disorders using cognitive-behavioural strategies. An initial paper by Aaron T. Beck in 1952 examined the potential of cognitive interventions for delusional beliefs. Subsequent to this, a number of small-scale studies (Chadwick & Lowe, 1990; Watts, Powell & Austin, 1973) served to maintain the interest in the ability of cognitive and behavioural interventions to impact on the symptoms of psychosis. However, the past decade has seen a growing interest in cognitive-behaviour therapy (CBT) for psychotic symptoms and a number of carefully conducted randomised-controlled trials have demonstrated the efficacy of this form of treatment (e.g. Drury et al., 1996; Kuipers et al., 1997; Sensky et al., 2000; Tarrier et al., 1998). In fact, on the basis of a meta-analysis of the data on the randomised-controlled trials to date, it has been suggested that not to provide CBT for psychosis would be unethical (Rector & Beck, 2001). It would seem, therefore, that to adopt an intervention that has proved so efficacious for people with established psychosis might also be useful in the developmental or prodromal stage. In Chapters 3 and 4, we will provide a full rationale for the use of CT with this client group.

This book has been written to reflect the experiences we have had over four years of working with people considered to be at high risk of developing psychosis. The 'Early Detection and Intervention Evaluation' (EDDIE) was started as a joint venture between the Bolton, Salford and Trafford Mental Health Trust, formerly Mental Health Services of Salford, and the University of Manchester (grantholders: A. P. Morrison and R. P. Bentall). The study was funded by the North West Regional NHS Executive R&D unit from 1999 to 2002, with additional funding obtained from the Stanley Foundation by S. W. Lewis. The study aimed to answer the following questions:

- Can we successfully identify a group at high risk of psychosis?
- Can we prevent or delay transition to psychosis using psychological intervention?
- Can we reduce the duration of untreated psychosis, should transition occur?
- Can we ameliorate psychosis, should transition occur?

The study was a single, blind, randomised-controlled trial. We have been encouraged by our results, which are to be reported elsewhere. Our findings have led to the development of a clinical service delivering early detection and CT, which is ongoing in Salford.

This book is intended to demonstrate the application of CT for individuals at high risk of developing psychosis in a clinician-friendly manner. Throughout the book, cases are utilised to demonstrate the application of techniques, and examples are provided to illustrate the points discussed. This work is in line with current clinical development guidelines such as the National Plan for the NHS and the National Service Framework (NSF) for Mental Health. It is also an area of growing research interest around the world, and it is hoped that this book will encourage others to evaluate the utility of psychological approaches to the prevention of psychosis.

The book is divided into three parts, with Part I focusing upon the background to this work, with chapters highlighting the rationale for this early intervention strategy, potential assessment strategies for identifying at-risk groups and a review of prevention strategies. This section incorporates the work of the early intervention pioneers (notably Patrick McGorry, Alison Yung and colleagues from Melbourne and Max Birchwood and colleagues in Birmingham).

In Part II, the focus is on the application of cognitive theory and therapy with this client group. Chapters in this section discuss the specifics of why CT is an ideal intervention for this client group, some of the practicalities associated with this kind of work, a cognitive theory of psychosis, and how the theory translates into idiosyncratic case formulations and assessment strategies.

Part III includes chapters that specifically examine strategies for change with this population. The first chapter focuses on normalisation strategies, building on the work of Kingdon and Turkington (1994). The next few chapters incorporate recent developments in CT (particularly the treatments for anxiety disorders developed by David M. Clark, Paul M. Salkovskis, Adrian Wells and colleagues) and discuss the process of generating and evaluating alternative beliefs, safety behaviours and metacognitive beliefs. The next chapter discusses specific core beliefs associated with people considered to be at risk for psychosis, which draws upon the work of Aaron T. Beck, Christine Padesky and colleagues, and chapters on social isolation and relapse prevention follow this. The final chapter draws together the themes developed throughout the book and considers future directions.

This is *not* a prescriptive treatment manual. It is not intended that the chapters specific to therapy in Part III be worked through one by one with each client. Rather, a formulation-based approach, where treatment strategies are selected on the basis of an idiosyncratic case conceptualisation, is encouraged. The various chapters in Part III represent many of the common themes and difficulties experienced by this client group and provide examples of how they may be tackled in therapy. However, this must be done within the context of a collaboratively derived formulation and related to the problems that are agreed and prioritised by the client.

PF

AM

ACKNOWLEDGEMENTS

We would like to thank the many colleagues who have influenced our work. These include cognitive theorists and therapists from the field of emotional disorders, such as Aaron T. Beck, David M. Clark, Ann Hackmann, Paul M. Salkovskis and Adrian Wells, in addition to those from the field of psychosis, such as Richard P. Bentall, Max Birchwood, Paul Chadwick, David Fowler, Andrew Gumley, Gillian Haddock, David Kingdon, Nick Tarrier and Douglas Turkington. We have also been heavily influenced by the work of the EPPIC and PACE services, including Pat McGorry, Alison Yung, Lisa Phillips and their colleagues. In addition, we would like to thank our colleagues in the IMPACT and EDIT teams in Salford and Trafford, who have supported us and made our working life enjoyable and interesting. Most importantly of all, we would like to thank our clients, who have taught us a lot about working with people at high risk of developing psychosis (in particular, Jenny Henry and Rory Byrne who continue to influence the development of our approach).

PF
AM

For my family: Delia, Chloe, Nadia and Ben.
PF

For Mel.
AM

BACKGROUND

PART I

BACKGROUND

THE IMPORTANCE OF EARLY RECOGNITION

RATIONALE

The length of time between the onset of psychotic symptoms and the subsequent detection, diagnosis and commencement of treatment has been termed the Duration of Untreated Psychosis (DUP) and is conceptualised as a treatment lag. The average length of DUP has been found to be approximately one year (Barnes et al., 2000; Beiser et al., 1993; Hafner et al., 1994; Loebel et al., 1992; McGorry et al., 1996) (see Figure 1.1). This is a fairly robust finding and these studies have been replicated in different countries and health settings indicating that the finding is generalisable. However, these studies report the mean DUP, which may lead to overestimates. If the median DUP is examined, then this gives a lower figure of 12 weeks (Drake et al., 2000). This indicates that DUP for the majority is around three months but some statistical outliers substantially increase the mean. Therefore DUP now tends to be calculated using both the mean and the median.

A number of studies have found that a longer DUP is associated with poorer prognosis (Crow et al., 1986; Loebel et al., 1992) and one study found it to be the most important predictor of treatment response in a large group of first admission patients (Drake et al., 2000). There are concerns that the association between DUP and poor treatment response may merely represent a difference in the illness itself with longer DUP being associated with a more insidious onset and shorter DUP associated with an acute presentation. A recent review of DUP (Norman & Malla, 2001) found that there is some tentative evidence to suggest a relationship between initial response to treatment and DUP, although they found no evidence to suggest a relationship to longer-term outcomes.

However, the main clinical implication from these findings is that minimising DUP would be advantageous to the client, their family and the treatment team even if this

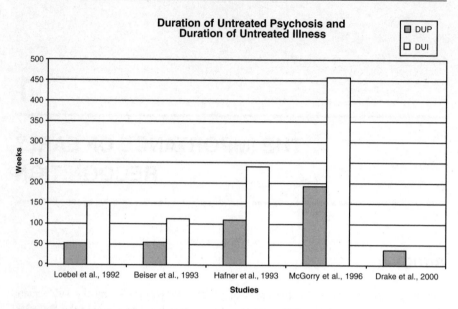

Figure 1.1   Duration of untreated psychosis and duration of untreated illness

were by a few weeks rather than months. Whatever definition is used, it is obvious that there are clear difficulties in being able to identify people who are in the early stages of psychosis, although a shorter DUP is associated with more frequent GP attendance in the six years before the onset of psychosis (Skeate et al., 2002). A recent study (Moller & Husby, 2000) interviewed people who had experienced their first psychotic episode and found that there may be factors associated with the symptoms themselves, which contribute to the DUP. In this study, two themes were found to be associated with a reluctance to disclose symptoms: one being a fear about disclosing symptoms because of what may happen; the second being that people become preoccupied with the symptoms and spend time encouraging them and engaging with them. Both fear and preoccupation can accentuate the DUP by preventing people from seeking assistance with these symptoms. However, it is not only the symptoms themselves which serve to prolong DUP. Unfortunately, as was found in the Northwick Park Study (Johnstone et al., 1986), if things are not managed in the early stages then deterioration continues until finally a crisis occurs, which frequently involves the police. This study found that people do try to access help for their symptoms, with an average of eight help-seeking contacts prior to appropriate treatment. Unfortunately, the police are often the final help-seeking contact, and it is often the police who act to initiate treatment. This will frequently involve taking the person for assessment, and this can often involve admission to hospital. These hospital admissions may be involuntary, requiring the use of the *Mental Health Act* in the UK. This whole process can be extremely traumatic for the individual, family and friends, and there is evidence that such admissions can lead to the development of post-traumatic stress disorder (e.g. Frame & Morrison, 2001; McGorry et al., 1991).

The timing of the onset of psychotic illness is frequently within the second and third decades of a person's life. This period is when people are starting to make their way in the world, developing relationships and careers, and many people in this age range may be considering the possibilities of starting a family. However, not only can the stress and sleep disturbance involved with bringing up children play a role in the development of psychosis, but also the onset of psychosis could significantly impact upon a developing parent–child relationship. Therefore, the onset of psychosis has the potential to interfere at this crucial stage in a person's development with the ability to impact not only on the individual, but also on family and friends.

Significantly, when working with people with an established psychotic illness, many interventions are aimed at reintegrating social contacts, assisting families in understanding the nature of psychosis or getting the person back to work or college. Interestingly, in the group who are at risk but who have not yet developed florid psychotic symptoms, many of these factors are still intact. People are still engaged in college courses or work and frequently have a range of social contacts and family support. Many of these things may be in the process of breaking down, but the individual and their family are often highly motivated to prevent this from happening. This can frequently be easier than having to start from a position where the person has lost these things and their confidence and self-esteem has been affected. For the person who develops distressing psychotic symptoms and does not have access to treatment, deterioration in family and social life can occur very quickly.

Therefore, this period of untreated psychosis can significantly impact on the individual, interfering with their psychological and social development. Frequently, symptoms of isolation and social anxiety are associated with psychosis (in some cases this may be due to concerns about stigma). Traditionally, social anxiety would be considered to be a co-morbid disorder or related to negative symptoms. However, it can be conceptualised as being on a continuum, where someone can move from social anxiety (or culturally acceptable concerns about interpersonal threat) to psychosis, such as paranoia (or culturally unacceptable concerns about interpersonal threat). In the initial stages of the development of psychosis, a person may start to isolate themselves from their peer group and, over time, friends may stop calling. Symptoms of paranoia can develop and this can affect the quality of relationships to the point where they may break down, which obviously increases the loss of contact with family and friends. These relationships can be vital not only for the usual benefits associated with friends, but also as learning opportunities for understanding how to develop social skills and manage social interaction. Therefore, their loss can be extremely damaging. Increased isolation can lead the individual towards increased risk of depression and suicide. Clearly, if isolation persists over any period of time this will impact on the individual's confidence in their ability to initiate and maintain social contacts, which can subsequently affect many aspects of their life. This can then become a secondary problem requiring treatment.

Another important area to consider at this point is how individuals may begin to cope with their emerging symptoms. Some people turn to alcohol or street drugs as a means of managing the distress they are experiencing, which can be a confounding factor. Unfortunately, most services tend to regard the drugs as being the cause of the psychosis. Therefore, they often believe that the drugs should be dealt with prior to the psychosis. It is certainly the case that drugs can induce psychotic experiences, although in our experience people frequently turn to drugs or alcohol as a means of reducing the distress or intensity of their developing psychotic symptoms (as a form of self-medication). Working with people with co-existing drug and alcohol use is, therefore, very important and the reasons for their use should be established rather than presumed.

All of these factors combine in the early stages of symptom development, conspiring to prevent early detection and treatment. However, as with many difficulties, the earlier a problem is identified and treatment is initiated, the easier it can be to treat. When symptoms are left for a long period of time they may become more resistant to treatment, and maintenance factors may become entrenched. Clearly, there are costs involved for the individual and family and an early identification approach could assist with some of these problems. Service providers and commissioners may be concerned about the costs of developing a proactive early detection and intervention service. However, they need to recognise that such a programme is likely to be cost effective (financially), as it is likely to reduce the number of people requiring admission to hospital (and such treatment is extremely expensive). Furthermore, it should be recognised that the personal and social costs of continuing with a reactive, crisis-driven approach to the recognition and management of psychosis is unacceptable (and the Department of Health guidelines (2001) suggest that this choice will no longer be an option in the UK). Working with individuals during the early stages of psychosis, in order to minimise the need for admission to hospital and coercive treatment, should be viewed positively by all concerned. However, it is important to offer a range of phase-specific interventions (Gleeson, Larsen & McGorry, 2003; Larsen, Bechdolf & Birchwood, 2003).

PREVENTION RATHER THAN CURE

The Duration of Untreated Illness (DUI) combines the initial prodromal period prior to the onset of psychosis and the DUP, with an average DUI being two years (see Figure 1.1). This indicates that there is a potential window of one year prior to the onset of psychosis during which people actively seek access to some form of help, often involving numerous unsuccessful presentations to services (Johnstone et al., 1986). Researchers in Australia have demonstrated that it is possible to identify people who may be at this stage, in what is considered to be an ultra high-risk or prodromal group (Yung et al., 1996). In one of their studies, they found that 40% of their high-risk sample became psychotic over a period of one year (Yung et al., 1998), which clearly demonstrates a high transition rate. Further work is being undertaken to refine assessment strategies for identifying these high-risk individuals (Klosterkotter et al., 2001; Miller & McGlashan, 2000; Morrison et al., 2002) in an effort to impact further on the ability to predict the onset of psychosis.

The idea behind the early identification of psychosis as a preventative strategy is not a particularly new one (Falloon, 1992; Sullivan, 1927). However, the Kraepelinian concept of psychosis, a rather hopeless view that has predominated for many years, has meant that researchers and services have been extremely slow to embrace the early intervention paradigm. Recently, the concept of a 'critical period' has been introduced which proposes that the early stages of the illness may offer an opportunity to maximise the effectiveness of our interventions (Birchwood, Todd & Jackson, 1998). In the UK, this approach is now considered a vital component of services for people with a psychotic illness (Department of Health, 2000, 2001). However, those people charged with supplying the funding for these types of innovative services are still struggling to provide what they consider core services such as community mental health teams or inpatient facilities. Unfortunately, there appears to be little recognition that if this approach was adopted it could significantly impact upon the need for these perceived core services. An early intervention strategy should be considered as one of these core services, which could then identify people earlier and offer preventative strategies with the potential to reduce some of the burden experienced by secondary services and the risk of iatrogenic damage to clients. Despite this, there are still some people who have their reservations (for a review of the arguments see the recent debate between Pelosi & Birchwood, 2003). The potential benefits of this approach would include: improved recovery (Birchwood & Macmillan, 1993); more rapid and complete remission (Loebel et al., 1992); better attitudes to treatment and lower levels of expressed emotion/family burden (Stirling et al., 1991); and less treatment resistance.

This book describes strategies developed to identify people at high risk of developing psychosis, and psychological interventions that have been developed in an attempt to prevent the transition to psychosis. The terms 'high risk' or 'at risk' will be utilised throughout the text as opposed to 'prodrome' or 'prodromal'; this is because the term 'prodrome' emphasises a pathological, as opposed to normalising, conceptualisation of the onset of psychosis, and it also implies that people are going to become psychotic (whereas the data would suggest that this is only accurate for a substantial minority).

2

HOW TO IDENTIFY AT-RISK GROUPS

INTRODUCTION

For some time, the strategies that have been used to identify those at risk of developing psychotic disorders have utilised the literature on genetic predisposition in order to inform their approach. This literature indicates that the chance of developing schizophrenia increases with genetic proximity to a person with a diagnosis of schizophrenia. Studies indicate that the prevalence in the general population is approximately 1:100 and this increases to 45:100 when both parents have a diagnosis of schizophrenia (Sham et al., 1994). Therefore, to use this strategy to identify high-risk groups would entail working with people who have a family history of a psychotic disorder and following them up over time. However, what this means is that even with both parents diagnosed with schizophrenia the future risk is 45% which means that 55% will clearly never go on to develop this disorder and therefore following them up over long periods of time could be extremely expensive and fruitless. Another important factor when considering this methodology is that very few people who develop schizophrenia have both parents diagnosed with this disorder. A recent paper pointed out that only 11% of cases of schizophrenia will have one or more parents with the same diagnosis, whilst 37% of all cases of schizophrenia will have neither a first- nor a second-degree relative with the same diagnosis (Gottesman & Erlenmeyer-Kimling, 2001). This means that if you were to use this single method of identifying cases by monitoring people with a first-degree family member you would miss out on nearly 90% of all future cases. Therefore, if this strategy were to be adopted, it would only identify a very specific subgroup of the population diagnosed with schizophrenia, which is now recognised as being a heterogeneous rather than homogeneous group.

MEASURES FOR DEFINING RISK

A number of assessment tools have been utilised to define high-risk individuals. In the early stages of this approach, established assessment tools that were designed for populations who had established psychotic symptoms were used. Currently, however, there are a number that have been designed specifically for the identification of high-risk individuals. Some of these measures have previously been reviewed (Halpin & Carr, 2000) although a number of the newer measures were not included in this review. At the present time, there are three measures that have been developed specifically for the identification of high-risk groups. These are the Comprehensive Assessment of At-Risk Mental States (CAARMS; Yung et al., 2000), the Bonn Scale for the Assessment of Basic Symptoms (BSABS; Klosterkotter et al., 2001) and the Structured Interview for Prodromal Symptoms and Scale of Prodromal Symptoms (SIPS/SOPS) (Miller et al., 1999). They have been generated from three centres around the world, the CAARMS being an Australian measure, the BSABS originating from Germany and the SIPS/SOPS from America. Prior to the emergence of these specific measures, researchers employed general measures which were designed for populations with established psychosis.

GENERAL MEASURES

The *Brief Psychiatric Rating Scale* (BPRS) (Overall & Gorham, 1962) and the *Positive and Negative Syndrome Scale* (PANSS) (Kay, Fiszbein & Opler, 1987) are well-established measures used in general psychiatry. The BPRS was originally utilised by Yung et al. (1998) in their research to identify high-risk groups. These measures are utilised to establish symptoms associated with psychotic disorders with an ability to measure frequency and severity of symptoms. The main disadvantage of the PANSS and the BPRS results from having been designed for a population with existing psychosis. They therefore lack sensitivity when measuring the developing psychotic symptoms associated with at-risk cases. The PANSS has been found to be an excellent tool in terms of reliability and criterion and construct validity (Kay, Opler & Lindenmayer, 1988) and has been reported as having superior interrater reliability and predictive validity in comparison with the BPRS (Bell et al., 1992). We have utilised the PANSS in our research, as other more specific tools were not validated at the time we commenced our work.

As mentioned previously, the PANSS does have limitations in the at-risk population in terms of its sensitivity for measuring developing symptoms. A great deal of the prompts associated with this measure assume that the person has experienced, or is experiencing, troubling psychotic symptoms, although this may not be the case with people who are considered at risk. Both the PANSS and the BPRS also include items relating to the measurement of insight, which in at-risk cases is problematic and may be inappropriate. Therefore, despite the BPRS and the PANSS being very useful tools for the assessment of actual psychosis and transition to psychosis they have clear limitations when used for this population as this is not the group they were originally designed for. Recently, alternatives have been developed based on the experiences of researchers working with this population.

MEASURES SPECIFIC TO AT-RISK POPULATIONS

Due to the current interest in early intervention strategies a number of researchers have devoted their efforts towards identification of ultra high-risk individuals. This has meant that specific measures have been developed which are suitable for this purpose and these various measures will now be discussed.

THE AUSTRALIAN GROUP

The approach we have chosen to adopt comes from the work undertaken in Melbourne, Australia, from the ORYGEN Youth Health service (formerly the Early Psychosis Prevention and Intervention Centre: EPPIC). Under the direction of Patrick McGorry, this group has been working with young people in the early stages of psychosis for over a decade and has pioneered much of the work in this area. It has a pragmatic approach and incorporates innovative treatments into mainstream services, evaluating its work and producing highly regarded and extremely influential research. This group now has a number of subgroups involved in providing services for young people, and one of these is the Personal Assessment and Crisis Evaluation (PACE) team, co-ordinated by Lisa Phillips.

One of the studies from this team, led by Alison Yung, examined a practical approach to identifying cases at a high risk of developing psychosis, which yielded a transition rate of 40% over a six-month period (Yung et al., 1996, 1998). This allows a pragmatic approach to case-identification incorporating a number of factors, which combine to leave the individual at risk of future psychosis over a relatively short period of time. One possible criticism of this study is that it is possible that people may have been psychotic at recruitment, but felt insufficiently comfortable to disclose this to the interviewer. This possibility is reinforced by the fact that, in the first six months of the study, eight cases made the transition to psychosis; however, five of these cases progressed to psychosis within the first month. Yung et al. (1998) do describe attempts to safeguard against this, however, and are confident that these cases were not psychotic at recruitment. Even if this proved to be the case, and people were actually psychotic rather than at risk, engaging people in this way identifies unrecognised first episodes of psychosis, and should, therefore, reduce DUP, which would be a legitimate target in its own right.

Risk Factors for Psychosis (the PACE Approach)

The strategy adopted by the PACE clinic in Melbourne is designed to identify ultra high-risk groups who are considered to be extremely vulnerable to psychosis within a short time frame. In order to achieve this, a number of factors need to be considered. The first important factor is age. Clearly, people of almost any age can develop

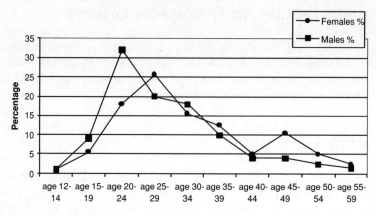

Figure 2.1 Graph demonstrating age of onset for schizophrenia
Source: adapted from Hafner et al. (1994)

psychotic symptoms. However, if adopting a strategy that is attempting to define an ultra high-risk group then we need to consider the age band in which the majority of people develop psychosis. This would include people between the ages of 14 and 30 (Yung et al., 1998), although recent recommendations from the Department of Health's *Early Intervention Policy Implementation Guide* (2001) in the UK suggest that services should target people aged 14–35. It is considered to be during this age range that the majority of people start to develop psychosis, as can be seen in Figure 2.1, and is therefore the first at-risk factor.

What is also evident from Figure 2.1 is the fact that males develop schizophrenia earlier in life than females, with the peak age of onset being around five years earlier for males than females (Hafner et al., 1994). However, the overall lifetime risk is approximately equal between the sexes (Jablensky et al., 1992). The graph also represents the point at which services acknowledge the onset of the disorder and qualify this with a diagnosis. It should be remembered that the person will have been experiencing difficulties for an average of approximately two years prior to this point if untreated illness and psychosis is taken into account.

Trait Factors

There is a general consensus amongst researchers and clinicians that a stress-vulnerability model best accounts for the available data relating to the aetiology of schizophrenia and related psychotic disorders (Gottesman, 1991; Gottesman & Shields, 1982; Nuechterlein & Dawson, 1984; Zubin & Spring, 1977). Stress-vulnerability models place a strong emphasis on biological or genetic vulnerability, which emphasises family history as a vulnerability factor. Therefore, if an individual has a first-degree relative with a history of any psychotic disorder and if the individual concerned is also experiencing stress, then they are considered to be at risk. Alternatively, if an individual is diagnosed with a schizophrenia spectrum disorder of schizotypal personality disorder and they are experiencing increased stress they would also be considered at risk. Therefore this is another factor associated with identifying a group at ultra high risk of psychosis. Yung et al. (1998) operationalised this by requiring either a first-degree relative with a diagnosis of a psychotic disorder, or a diagnosis of schizotypal personality disorder in the presenting individual, *plus* a recent deterioration in functioning, which they operationalised using the Global Assessment of Functioning (GAF) (American Psychiatric Association, 1994).

State Factors

As discussed, the majority of people who develop psychosis have no immediate family history of it. Therefore, a symptom-based approach to identification can be employed for this population. This approach relies on the fact that psychotic symptoms do not emerge fully formed overnight. Instead the approach from the PACE clinic describes two categories of high risk as being (1) attenuated psychotic symptoms and (2) Brief Limited Intermittent Psychotic Symptoms (BLIPS) (Yung et al., 1998). The category of attenuated symptoms describes a population with sub-clinical psychotic experiences. The BLIPS category classifies individuals as high risk if they have experienced frank psychotic symptoms that resolved spontaneously within a week (without recourse to treatment). In this category, it is assumed that the individual may experience further BLIPS and the space between the BLIPS decreases until again they develop frank psychotic symptoms.

In the early work from PACE the BPRS was used to define these symptom-based criteria. The PACE group has subsequently developed the *Comprehensive Assessment of At-Risk Mental States* (CAARMS). This is a measure that has drawn upon their research findings and clinical experience to produce a tool, which incorporates all of the state and trait characteristics in one simple measure. It also incorporates a number of refinements including more appropriate probes to elicit at-risk symptoms rather than relying on the established measures.

THE GERMAN GROUP

During the 1960s, Gerd Huber examined longitudinal studies of schizophrenia (Huber et al., 1980) and the idea of 'basic symptoms' was developed (Gross et al., 1989) from this retrospective standpoint. These symptoms aided the identification of symptoms associated with the early course of the illness and are operationalised in the *Bonn Scale for the Assessment of Basic Symptoms* (BSABS). A recent study has used the

BSABS as a predictive instrument (Klosterkotter et al., 2001), and reported that 70% of a clinic sample of 110 subjects who had endorsed one or more items on the BSABS had developed DSM-IV schizophrenia at 9.6-year follow-up. These findings indicate a clear ability to identify high-risk populations and at face value would be a strong argument for the adoption of this measure. However, this finding is specifically related to a population referred to psychiatry. If it were used in the general population it is envisaged that a large number of false negatives would be identified due to the nature of some of the items in the measure. It has been suggested that instead of 70% of individuals going on to develop a psychotic disorder the figures would be more like 2%, and therefore the measure would have limited value when translated to this setting (Warner, 2002). Pragmatically, to achieve these results also requires that the person be followed up over an extended period of time, and these factors combine to limit the use of this measure to clinical populations at the present time. Research is currently underway to examine the efficacy of this measure in general populations through the European Predication of Schizophrenia (EPOS) study.

THE AMERICAN GROUP

In America there has been growing interest in the ability to predict at-risk cases and Thomas McGlashan and his colleagues have been involved in a number of research projects around the world. His group has developed the *Structure Interview for Prodromal Symptoms* (SIPS) *and Scale of Prodromal Symptoms* (SOPS) at the PRIME clinic (Miller et al., 1999). This is a specific tool that has been developed for the assessment of at-risk cases and draws heavily on the work undertaken by Yung and colleagues in Australia. The SIPS/SOPS has been used in a large randomised trial in America and is currently being utilised in a large trial in Europe (the EPOS study). It has been translated into at least 12 different languages for use around the world; therefore, there should soon be a great deal of data regarding this measure. It has clear advantages over the general measures, in that it has a higher degree of sensitivity for detecting and measuring signs associated with at-risk cases. The probes used to elicit symptoms are also more appropriate to at-risk groups and transition to psychosis is easily calculated.

THE EDDIE APPROACH (ENGLAND)

We have operationalised this high-risk population using an adaptation of Yung et al.'s (1998) duration and severity criteria, which we based on Positive and Negative Symptoms Scale (PANSS) cut-off scores. This is because, at the time we commenced our research, none of the specific measures were available. Sub-clinical, attenuated psychotic symptoms were defined with the presence of symptoms that score 3 on delusions, 2–3 on hallucinations, 3–4 on suspiciousness or 3–4 on conceptual disorganisation. Alternatively, experiences that have been termed Brief Limited Intermittent

Psychotic Symptoms (BLIPS) are defined with the presence of symptoms that score 4 or more on hallucinations, 4 or more on delusions, or 5 or more on conceptual disorganisation, last less than one week and resolve without antipsychotic medication.

We operationally defined trait-plus-state risk factors in a similar manner to Yung et al. (1998). Our criteria used the presence of an at-risk mental state [defined for the purposes of our study as meeting caseness on the General Health Questionnaire (GHQ) (Goldberg & Hillier, 1979) and/or a recent deterioration in function of 30 points or more on the GAF] plus either a genetic risk indicated by a first-degree relative with a history of any psychotic disorder *or* a diagnosis of schizotypal personality disorder in the participant.

SCORING GUIDELINES FOR IDENTIFICATION OF AT-RISK GROUPS

Figure 2.2 illustrates the scores relating to the measures we utilise for defining an individual as being at high risk of developing psychosis according to PANSS criterion.

THE PROCESS OF IDENTIFICATION

It is impractical to expect the majority of people who come into contact with at-risk clients to have access to, and be able to utilise, the complex assessment tools available to assess at-risk populations. However, it is important that individuals from many different settings have some method for making decisions about relative risk of psychosis. In our experience, it is necessary to invest a large amount of time and energy in liaising with a wide range of potential referral sources. In Figure 2.3, the majority of agencies approached who may come into contact with at-risk or prodromal individuals are listed. It is important to allocate sufficient time to developing referral pathways with such diverse agencies, given the wide variety of pathways to care.

The initial stage involves contacting each of the various agencies; at this time, it is necessary to speak to managers of services in order to gain the confidence of, and access to, such organisations. However, it is just as important to access the general workforce who will have more direct contact with individuals who may be at risk. Therefore, if at all possible, meetings with both managers and frontline staff should take place, which obviously take extra time, but often prove extremely worthwhile. This usually involves provision of education to potential referrers, consisting of information about what symptoms or features to look for. Material should always be left for future reference, in order to guide decision-making regarding the potential onset of psychosis. One of the guides for referrers that we have developed is shown in Figure 2.4 (a larger version is included as Appendix 8 on p. 134). It is important that

State risk factors	
ATTENUATED SYMPTOMS GROUP	BLIPS GROUP
Rating on PANSS • 2 or 3 on hallucinations *or* • 3+ on delusions *or* • 3–4 on suspiciousness *or* • 3–4 on conceptual disorganisation The symptoms experienced should occur with a frequency of several times per week and change in mental state be present for one week	Rating on PANSS • 4+ on hallucinations *or* • 4+ on delusions *or* • 5+ on suspiciousness The symptoms experienced should be present for less than one week prior to spontaneous resolution
Trait risk factors	
• Those clients with a first-degree relative with a history of psychosis *and* • Caseness on the GHQ *or* • Loss of 30 points or more on GAF	• Those clients who meet criteriafor schizotypal personality disorder DSM-IV *and* • Caseness on the GHQ *or* • Loss of 30 points or more on GAF

Figure 2.2   Table demonstrating PANSS criteria for defining at-risk groups

this guide is easily understood, allows for a range of potential routes into psychosis and enables people to feel happy about referring cases, which may, or may not, be at-risk cases. This has been adapted from the work of Launer and MacKean (2000).

If this process is undertaken it can generate referrals, encouraging people to be aware of the potential onset of psychosis. Following referral, the individual is then seen by one of the early detection team who are aware of, and have expertise in, the assessment of at-risk cases, which will be discussed in the next section. This provides a screening service for the at-risk population.

IDENTIFICATION OF CASES

Our project aimed to determine if it was possible to identify a high-risk population in the British Health Care System using similar criteria to those developed in Melbourne

Schools
Colleges
Universities
Voluntary services
Social services
GPs
Primary care teams
Accident and emergency services
Community mental health teams
Adolescent mental health teams

Figure 2.3   Potential referral sources

(Morrison et al., 2002). During the project, we had 134 people referred. Of the 134, 27 did not meet criteria, 4 were already taking antipsychotic medication (an exclusion criterion), 14 already met DSM-IV criteria for psychosis, and 28 did not attend assessment appointments. Of the 61 remaining, 3 declined to consent to randomisation (2 wanted to remain with their existing counsellors and not risk randomisation to a monitoring-only condition). This meant that a final total of 58 were randomised to monitoring or treatment plus monitoring.

The fact that nearly 10% of the total sample were already psychotic demonstrates the utility of early detection strategies in recognising first episodes of psychosis and minimising DUP. This has also been the case in a number of other teams in the UK with the EDIT team (Early Detection and Intervention Team) in Birmingham and the OASIS team in London finding that closer to 25% of their referrals are already psychotic. Many of those found to be psychotic had been viewed as not warranting interventions for psychosis by existing (frequently secondary) health services. If an unrecognised first episode is detected, then members of the project staff advocate on behalf of the client in order to access services for their problems and ensure appropriate treatment is provided. This, in itself, is an important function for any early detection team.

In order to identify such cases, a large amount of time was spent raising the profile of the team. Presentations to key potential sources of referral were undertaken. Someone from our team would then attempt to keep in touch with an identified person from the referral source, in order to regularly prompt them about referral criteria. Initially, presentations were made to GPs and Community Mental Health Teams (CMHTs).

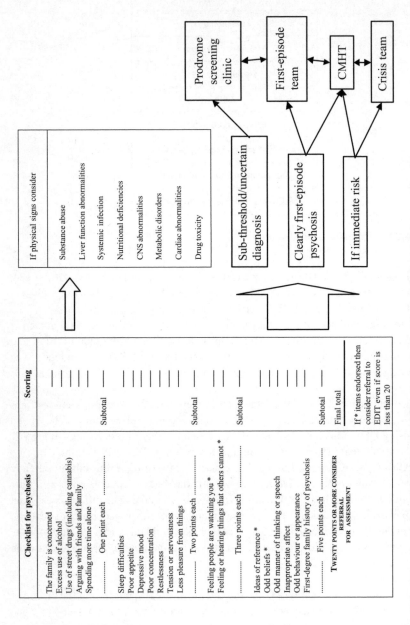

Checklist for psychosis | **Scoring**

The family is concerned | |
Excess use of alcohol | |
Use of street drugs (including cannabis) | |
Arguing with friends and family | |
Spending more time alone | |
.... One point each .... | Subtotal

Sleep difficulties | |
Poor appetite | |
Depressive mood | |
Poor concentration | |
Restlessness | |
Tension or nervousness | |
Less pleasure from things | |
.... Two points each .... | Subtotal

Feeling people are watching you * | |
Feeling or hearing things that others cannot * | |
.... Three points each .... | Subtotal

Ideas of reference * | |
Odd beliefs * | |
Odd manner of thinking or speech | |
Inappropriate affect | |
Odd behaviour or appearance | |
First-degree family history of psychosis | |
.... Five points each .... | Subtotal

Final total |

TWENTY POINTS OR MORE CONSIDER REFERRAL FOR ASSESSMENT

If * items endorsed then consider referral to EDIT even if score is less than 20

If physical signs consider

Substance abuse
Liver function abnormalities
Systemic infection
Nutritional deficiencies
CNS abnormalities
Metabolic disorders
Cardiac abnormalities
Drug toxicity

Sub-threshold/uncertain diagnosis → Prodrome screening clinic

Clearly first-episode psychosis → First-episode team

If immediate risk

First-episode team ↔ CMHT ↔ Crisis team

Figure 2.4 Primary care guidelines for identification of suspected or first-episode psychosis
Source: adapted from Launer & MacKean (2000)

However, as we progressed, the names of other organisations that may come into contact with at-risk individuals were passed to the team. It was not feasible to have face-to-face contact with every GP, so presentations were arranged at local postgraduate medical meetings, and visits were made to larger practices where a number of GPs could be present. However, every GP in the area was sent information about the project with a symptom checklist to indicate criteria for at-risk mental states, and details of how to refer clients.

Schools and colleges were extremely reluctant to allow us to talk to them, and we were unable to present our study in any of these organisations. We were uncertain of the reasons behind this, although the people we contacted discussed being extremely busy and also appeared to be concerned about discussing potential mental health problems (and especially psychosis) within their schools. It is important to note that we were not asking to go and talk to the children but to the staff group; however, they remained sceptical about what we were doing. University counsellors also had reservations about the project in the initial stages, although they did agree to meet with us and allow us to explain the project in detail. Once the university counsellors started to refer, they found that it was benefiting their clients, which stimulated further referrals. They eventually became one of our largest sources of referrals. They reported that the project was extremely useful, primarily for their clients, but also for themselves as clinicians when they were confused and unsure of what to do with an at-risk client. Regular planned contact was maintained with the university counsellors in case they experienced any difficulties regarding the project, and this was felt to be a useful process. This model was then adopted for the various agencies we became involved with so that when a member of the EDDIE team presented to a group of people from an agency, regular contact was maintained afterwards, frequently with an interested member of that team. Because of the nature of services and pathways to care for psychosis, it was necessary for the EDDIE team to present to a wide range of organisations including: various social services departments; education providers (particularly universities); voluntary sector services; and a range of health providers. This is illustrated in the referral rates that are shown in Figure 2.5.

The process of accessing these services was felt to be extremely important. Initially, speaking to managers of a service is obviously vital as previously discussed; however, in our experience, we found that a further presentation should be arranged for those people who had regular contact with the client group. It is important not to be swayed by managers who say they will cascade the information down; this task should be undertaken by the early detection service. This is because, in many cases, managers are extremely busy and may allocate only a small amount of time to undertake this task. In our experience, if it was left to managers there was a possibility of the presentation being diluted because of competing demands, reduced conviction about the project, lack of understanding about reasons behind the project, uncertainty about referral criteria, or uncertainty about the referral process. Therefore, if at all possible, we would attempt to undertake this ourselves, emphasising the fact that it would be one less task for the manager.

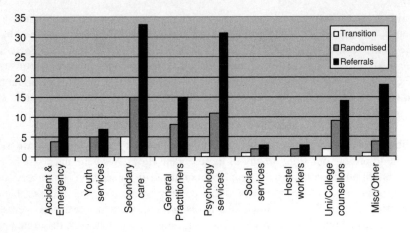

Figure 2.5 Graph demonstrating referrals and suitability

The process of referral was simplified in order to enable easy access to the service. Lengthy referral forms were avoided, as this can be a barrier to someone contacting a service, particularly if the referrer is concerned about the client's presenting difficulties. Referrers were advised that they could contact the team by letter, phone or email. We encouraged people to be over-inclusive with referrals, rather than under-inclusive, and emphasised that we could be utilised as a screening service for people. Several of the voluntary organisations commented that they felt somewhat reluctant to refer to some health organisations because they would frequently feel intimidated by them. These organisations described the fact that they would be asked detailed questions, often using terminology they found difficult to follow, and reported that this could affect their use of services, potentially delaying referral until a more obvious, clearly defined problem had emerged. We attempted to overcome this at presentations by discussing the fact that all the team would try to adopt a user-friendly approach, not just with the client, but also with the referring organisation. The team would then try to assess the new referral within one week of receiving it, although this is dependent on availability of the client and a suitable venue for them to be seen. The client would be assessed in a negotiated location and at a negotiated time. All clients were seen away from secondary care settings and in their own locality, thereby minimising the distance they had to travel. The quickest response to a referral was six hours, the time taken from receiving the referral to the individual being assessed and accepted as suitable.

TRANSITION RATES

In the EDDIE study, a total of 134 referrals were generated from a variety of different sources, and the relative accuracy of referrals and those that went on to make transition to psychosis can also be seen in Figure 4.1 (see page 35). Overall, 10 patients (17%) were defined as having made transition according to PANSS criteria, prescription of antipsychotic medication or DSM-IV diagnosis of a psychotic disorder. However, we found that transition rates were significantly reduced in the CT group, in comparison with the group that received monitoring alone (for further details, see Morrison et al., 2003).

SUMMARY

The ability to predict psychosis-prone individuals has been of interest to researchers and clinicians for many years, with efforts previously focusing upon the theories of genetic predisposition. Recently, a more pragmatic approach has been developed in Australia, in which symptom-based indicators, alongside family history, are utilised in an effort to identify a group who are considered to be ultra high risk over a relatively short period of time. This concept has been developing over the last few years, originally relying on established tools designed for use with people with schizophrenia; however, these tools have distinct limitations. Currently, there are new measures, which have been developed specifically for the purpose of identifying people considered to be at ultra high risk of future psychosis. However, the process of identifying at-risk cases can be similar to finding a needle in a haystack – these cases present in many different ways and through many different pathways to care. It is important, therefore, to encourage referrals from a wide range of sources, in order to allow for this diversity in presentation. If sufficient time is allocated to developing this complex referral system, then it is possible to identify such cases.

3

WHICH PREVENTION STRATEGY TO ADOPT

PREVENTION STRATEGIES

Mrazek and Haggerty (1994) have discussed the idea of preventative interventions and identified three prevention strategies. These are:

- universal
- selective, and
- indicated.

These will now be discussed in more detail.

Universal Strategies

If a universal strategy were to be adopted, then this would require a whole population to be inoculated against a disease or disorder. There are a number of preventative interventions that adopt this approach for specific diseases such as the measles, mumps and rubella (MMR) vaccine, which is given to children to prevent the onset of these diseases. It is then hoped that the vaccine is taken up by the population as a whole in an effort to eradicate the disease. A universal strategy aimed at the prevention of psychosis could be to administer a low-dose neuroleptic medication through the domestic drinking water system in a similar way that fluoride is added in an attempt to minimise tooth decay. This strategy would then treat the whole population with this low dose of neuroleptic in an attempt at inoculation. However, there is a possibility that this strategy may raise some ethical concerns. A psychological approach to this universal strategy of inoculation might be to educate the whole population about psychosis, which is potentially an important consideration, although the effectiveness of an educational intervention alone is likely to have limited success in preventing transition to psychosis. However, it probably presents fewer ethical dilemmas than putting neuroleptic medication into public drinking water.

Selective Strategies

The selective intervention approach, as discussed by Mrazek and Haggerty (1994), would target those individuals who were exposed to specific risk factors. In relation to psychosis, this would encompass those with a genetic predisposition (i.e. those people with a family history of psychosis). This group could then be targeted with interventions, whether medical or psychological, in an attempt to prevent transition to psychosis. However, as we have already discussed, this would serve to identify only a small and specific subgroup of those people who go on to develop psychosis. Therefore, this strategy alone is not an effective means of managing this problem.

Indicated Strategies

The final approach, and the one which is utilised in this text, would be to target those people who are felt to be at high risk and who display minimal, but detectable, signs of psychosis. This approach has been termed 'indicated prevention' and is the strategy adopted by the PACE clinic. The approach of Yung and colleagues has been adopted by a number of research projects around the world, which use similar strategies for the identification of at-risk cases, based on their criteria. However, the treatment options following the identification of cases are radically different.

WHICH INTERVENTION?

There are a variety of approaches that have been taken to the indicated prevention of psychosis. In Australia, in their early work, Yung et al. (1998) utilised support-ive psychosocial interventions. Despite these interventions, they still found transition rates of 40%. Without these interventions, it is possible that transition rates could have been higher still. This led to the conclusion that psychological interventions by themselves may not be that potent in terms of reducing transition to psychosis. This has led to a randomised-controlled trial (McGorry et al., 2002) to test the ability of specific interventions to reduce transition rates. In this trial, their specific interven-tions include medication (low-dose risperidone) and cognitive-behavioural therapy as interventions, which they consider may have some specificity in preventing transition to psychosis. These interventions were chosen due to their efficacy with existing psy-chotic symptoms. In the trial, these interventions are compared against Needs Based Interventions (NBI), which include case management, education and supportive psy-chotherapy targeted at the presenting symptoms. In this trial, they randomised 59 patients, 28 to the NBI group and 31 to the specific intervention group. At the end of the treatment phase, which lasted for six months, there was a significant difference in transition rates between the specific intervention group and the NBI group. However, after six months follow-up, the difference was no longer significant (0.24) when using an intention to treat analysis. They conclude that this indicates that it is possible to delay onset of psychosis, and hints at the possibility of preventing transition to psychosis.

In America, they have utilised a similar identification strategy, based on the approach pioneered by Yung and colleagues, although they have developed the SIPS and SOPS (Miller & McGlashan, 2000) as specific measures to assist with the identification of at-risk cases rather than relying on more general measures. They have adopted a medical intervention, choosing an atypical antipsychotic medication (olanzapine) as their primary intervention. The study is a double-blind randomised-controlled trial (McGlashan et al., 2003). Participants are randomly allocated to receive either a placebo or olanzapine. This is taken for one year, which is followed by a further year of assessment with no medication. If the person makes the transition to psychosis then the blind is immediately broken and olanzapine is prescribed. This is a multi-site trial and has randomised 60 patients who were deemed to be at risk according to the SIPS.

The current position regarding medication seems to be that of clinical equipoise (McGorry et al., 2002), which means that there is insufficient research evidence either way to determine whether medication is justifiable with at-risk clients (which is exactly what some of the studies are trying to determine). Some believe that the emergence of sub-clinical symptoms, heralding an at-risk mental state, warrants the use of neuroleptic medication, whilst others believe that the initiation of neuroleptic medication in at-risk cases may expose large numbers of false positives to side effects of these medications unnecessarily, given the current accuracy of measures of risk (Bentall & Morrison, 2002). Bentall and Morrison (2002) also argue that the use of antipsychotic medication with this population risks intervening with psychotic experiences that cause no distress and may be valued by the person (or even functional). They also suggest that the distressing side effects of antipsychotic medication, including the newer atypicals, which commonly produce weight gain and sexual dysfunction, should be considered. Such side effects can have significant impact on self-esteem, especially in the age group in which many of the at-risk cases fall, and antipsychotic medications can still cause neuroleptic malignant syndrome, which can be fatal. Significantly, if medication is prescribed and it transpires that side effects are experienced, then there is the potential for this to adversely affect engagement with services in the future. Bentall and Morrison (2002) also note that the effects of such medication on the developing brains of adolescents are currently unknown. Such considerations make such pharmacological interventions problematic.

We believe that medication in at-risk cases is not justifiable as a first line of intervention, as large numbers of young people defined as being high risk will not make the transition to psychosis. If all of them are prescribed medication then a large number will be exposed to the side effects of the medication without the requirement for this. Indeed, McGorry et al.'s (2002) data certainly suggests that CT is a more acceptable intervention than even very low-dose antipsychotic medication, and they suggest (p. 926) that:

> Some patients could be treated with psychological therapy alone as a first-line strategy.

It is important not to assume that a psychological intervention is exempt from side effects. If a treatment can bring about positive change, then it is also possible that it will bring about negative changes. An obvious risk of intervening with an at-risk population is the possibility of unnecessary stigmatisation. The terminology used is also likely to be an issue in relation to this; it would seem to be needlessly stigmatising, not to mention inaccurate given the false positives, to regard a high-risk population as 'prodromal', 'pre-psychotic' or 'pre-schizophrenic'. Rather, describing the population as 'distressed', 'help-seeking' and 'at risk of developing psychosis' would seem to be more accurate and less likely to pathologise or stigmatise individuals.

SUMMARY

Initially the impetus behind identification of individuals at high risk was an attempt to monitor these individuals as this could facilitate early treatment if the individual makes transition to psychosis, thereby reducing DUP. Since this has now become a possibility, consideration of treatments, which could be utilised as a first-line, primary preventative measure to halt the course of psychosis, have been examined. In many ways, the strategy that is chosen once high-risk individuals are identified is vital to the whole issue surrounding the early identification of high-risk cases. The treatment strategy chosen should be acceptable to the client and have the ability to target their specific problems. If the treatment strategy is not effective, or has side effects that may prevent the individual from taking up the intervention, then this will obviously have implications. It has been remarked that pharmacological interventions with neuroleptic medications would not have been considered prior to the emergence of the atypical drugs. However, even the atypical preparations still have a range of side effects which, whilst not as disabling as the older antipsychotic agents, can still be intolerable (particularly to someone who has less than a 50% chance of developing psychosis). Due to the nature of prodromal symptoms, a psychological approach appears to be an optimal treatment, which can target not only emerging psychotic symptoms, but also associated difficulties such as anxiety and depression, which may have led to their help-seeking behaviour. Of the psychological interventions available, cognitive therapy (CT) appears to be the treatment of choice, and the rationale for this will be discussed in Chapter 4.

PART II

COGNITIVE THERAPY FOR PREVENTION OF PSYCHOSIS

4

WHY COGNITIVE THERAPY?

WHY COGNITIVE THERAPY?

Several arguments can be adduced to suggest that CT may be particularly beneficial to high-risk groups. First, the psychological processes typically targeted during CT include metacognitions and self-schemas, factors that we have shown to be elevated in people at risk of psychosis (Morrison et al., 2002). Second, it has been shown in established psychotic patients that cognitive-behavioural monitoring of prodromal signs can facilitate early intervention and relapse prevention or amelioration (Birchwood et al., 1989), and provision of CT to people at risk of relapse significantly reduces relapses and hospital admissions (Gumley et al., 2003). This suggests that CT will be of use to those who have experienced BLIPS.

Similarly, there are a number of randomised-controlled trials that have indicated the efficacy of cognitive-behavioural interventions for acute and chronic psychotic symptoms in patients with schizophrenia-spectrum diagnoses (Drury et al., 1996; Kuipers et al., 1997; Sensky et al., 2000; Tarrier et al., 1998). If CT is effective in reducing distress associated with persistent psychotic symptoms, then it is likely that CT will be of use to those who are experiencing attenuated psychotic symptoms. Another compelling rationale for the provision of cognitive-behaviour therapy (CBT) to people at high risk of developing psychosis is the predominance of mood-related symptoms in psychotic prodromal states (Birchwood, 1996). CBT is an effective treatment for both anxiety disorders (e.g. Clark, 1999) and depression (e.g. Hollon et al., 1996). Therefore, it is likely that CT will help with the common emotional disorders that are present in a high-risk population. For example, McGorry et al. (2002) reported that of the 43 cases in their trial who did not make transition to psychosis, 8 met criteria for a mood disorder (major depressive disorder or dysthymia) and 8 cases met criteria for an anxiety disorder. It is also likely that the format of CT, which emphasises the development of shared problem lists and goals, will ensure that it can be useful to the 'false positives'. This format also means that CT can target any concerns about stigma, given that there is a possibility of stigmatisation arising from being labelled as high risk or from their behaviour. When considered together, these arguments suggest that CBT may be uniquely suitable for preventing transition to psychosis in a way that is acceptable to clients and their carers.

WHAT FORM SHOULD THE COGNITIVE THERAPY TAKE?

How CT is delivered, whether in groups, individually or in the form of family-based interventions, is a matter for further research. Group-based interventions could potentially be a powerful intervention for this population. Group members could undertake much of the work and normalisation of experiences should be easily achieved. Despite this, the high-risk population is not homogeneous. Their problems vary considerably; therefore, developing a group cognitive intervention that could embrace a multitude of problems could prove difficult. Also, engagement for a group-based intervention could be problematic. Those at high risk are not the easiest population to identify, and it is possible that some people identified would not want to take part in a group intervention as these could be perceived as being more threatening. Therefore, it may prove difficult to get enough people together at one time, who are willing to participate in a group. Our service offers a group approach, which is co-facilitated by a former service user, in addition to individual therapy.

Family interventions in psychosis have demonstrated their efficacy (Pharoah, Mari & Striener, 2000; Tarrier et al., 1988, 1994), albeit primarily within well-conducted and resourced research programmes. However, despite numerous training programmes, the implementation of these interventions following training is still quite limited (Fadden, 1997). It is also important to consider the nature of these interventions, which frequently involve a psychoeducational component, and focus on the fact that a member of the family has schizophrenia. The education then reinforces the fact that schizophrenia is a disabling illness that will require long-term treatment, including medication. This is somewhat at odds with the message that is emphasised within our approach to working with high-risk clients. However, it is frequently necessary to engage with family members in order to provide support for them as well. Family interventions specific to at-risk groups will require further development. This leaves the individual approach, which pragmatically appears to be most appropriate. This approach has been discussed briefly elsewhere (French et al., 2001, 2003); however, we wish to expand on previous descriptions of the therapy process. In this next section we will focus on the structure and process of the intervention in more detail.

INDIVIDUAL COGNITIVE THERAPY

The specific ingredients of CT are somewhat different according to which disorder is being treated. However, there are clearly some aspects of CT that remain constant.

According to Beck (1976), CT should:

- be based upon a cognitive model which describes the onset and maintenance of the disorder being treated
- be formulation driven
- be a structured process
- be based on shared problems and goals
- be educational, allowing the client to understand the process of therapy
- utilise guided discovery as the engine for change
- involve homework tasks; and
- be time limited.

Based on a Cognitive Model

CT should be based upon a cognitive model of the disorder being treated. This allows the development of testable case conceptualisations that can be used to select treatment strategies. There are several cognitive models describing the onset and maintenance of psychosis; however, our approach utilises the model of psychosis outlined by Morrison (2001), which is described in detail in Chapter 6.

Formulation Driven

The difference between providing cognitive techniques and CT is that, in the latter, the cognitive therapist selects and applies strategies for change, which are driven by the formulation of an individual's problems. A formulation is developed early in therapy based on the cognitive model that informs the specific disorder. It provides a strategy for dealing with the problems. However, it is vital a case formulation is seen as a dynamic process that can grow and change throughout therapy. The therapist should not stick rigidly to their initial conceptualisation if it does not seem to fit, and the formulation should be regularly reviewed throughout the therapy process.

Structure

Having structure to the sessions is seen as an important aspect of CT (Beck et al., 1979; Liese & Franz, 1996) and enables the client and therapist to start to work together by systematically reviewing the problems and planning appropriate goals and strategies to achieve them. Structure is there to maximise the contact time and ensure that all points the client and therapist wish to cover are achieved. This involves a socialisation process where the therapist socialises the client not only to the model of how thoughts influence feelings and behaviours, but also of how imposing a structure to work with those thoughts can be extremely productive. There are differences of opinion regarding the importance of structure in CT with psychosis (see, for example, Fowler, Garety & Kuipers, 1995; Morrison et al., 2003). We would argue that, when working with a pre-psychotic client group, the usual structure of CT should be adhered to.

EXAMPLE

A counsellor had seen a client for approximately a year before being referred to our project. This client was seen for eight CT sessions. At the end of the treatment he was approached about what he felt was helpful about therapy, and part of his response was:

> *The structure was really important, instead of letting me just ramble on about things, which can be okay at times, we actually focused in on the problems and dealt with them. I suppose I felt that I would always be in some kind of therapy but I feel fine now, no problems and I could not have imagined that.*

Shared Problems and Goals

The development of a problem list is of vital importance. This will allow the client to have some direction over his/her therapy (Kirk, 1989), contributing to the collaborative nature of CT. There are several key steps in providing problem-orientated interventions, which should be based around these principles (Hawton & Kirk, 1989):

1. Identify the problem
2. Translate this into a goal
3. Identify strengths
4. Draw on strengths – find a realistic way to the goal
5. Set a realistic goal

Below are a number of examples of items from the problem lists of our clients:

'I am unhappy with where I live'
'I feel anxious when I leave the house'
'I want to find my real mother'
'I worry about people laughing at me when I go out'
'I need to get a job'
'I want more money'
'My sister is nasty to me'
'I want to stop it happening to me again'
'I want to know what is wrong with me'
'I feel depressed'
'I feel anxious'
'I need a girlfriend'

Many of these items come up on problem lists repeatedly in some form or another.

Common themes from problem lists include:

- loneliness
- social anxiety
- lack of a confidante
- perceiving self to be different
- symptoms indicate 'going mad'
- metacognition
- trauma
- accommodation difficulties

Intervention strategies related to some of these themes will be examined in more detail in the subsequent chapters.

Once an exhaustive problem list is generated it should be translated into a goal. It is important that the goals are written in behavioural terms in order that the client can actually see if goals are attained. A goal statement such as *I would like to feel happier/better* should be operationalised through additional questioning such as: *If you were happier what would you be doing?*

The goals should be written according to the following (SMART) format:

Specific
Measurable
Achievable
Realistic
Time Limited

The process of moving towards specific therapy goals from a series of daunting problems can be a lengthy process. It may well take one or two full sessions in order to properly complete the task. This may seem to be an inordinate amount of what is fairly limited therapy time, but the process can be extremely therapeutic in itself. Collaboratively developing specific goals to work on may be the first time that the client has sat down and tried to work out the specifics of their problems and see that goals can be attainable. Also, problems are negative, and in the past or present, whereas goals are positive, and in the future.

EXAMPLES OF GOALS

- To find out what alternative accommodation is available and send letters or contact by phone the various housing agencies in order to get on their waiting lists

- When I go out, I would like to be able to distinguish with more certainty if people are laughing at me, or whether I just feel this is the case (and preferably reduce distress from 60 to 30%)
- To begin to understand if what I am experiencing is the start of schizophrenia
- If I felt less anxious I would like to be able to leave the house and go to the local shops when I felt like it (and at least three times a week)

Educational

A significant emphasis in CT is placed on enabling the individual to understand the process of therapy. The educational component is associated with teaching the individual to understand and formulate their own problems and devise ways of evaluating their thoughts, generating alternative explanations and testing out their fears. This process, which enables the individual to become their own therapist, can be a major factor in reducing rates of relapse. The structured nature of therapy assists this process.

Guided Discovery

A principle feature associated with CT is the use of Socratic dialogue in order to achieve guided discovery. This questioning style has been considered as the engine, which drives CT. It requires the therapist to be highly active within therapy and fosters collaborative empiricism. The process involves the therapist asking questions, which enable the client to evaluate the advantages and disadvantages of their thinking processes and the accuracy of their thoughts. It is not about the therapist being challenging or using persuasion in order to convince the client that they need to see things differently, but rather should be about a shared journey of discovery. This questioning style is a vital component of therapy and should be an integral part of the therapy process.

Homework

This is an integral aspect of CT and should be considered as such. This means allocating specific time on the agenda in order to set homework and to evaluate homework that has been undertaken since the previous session. The rationale for homework should be clearly explained to the individual and the selection of homework tasks should reflect what has been discussed in session. A rationale for homework is presented below:

> *Clearly, we will only meet for about one hour, once a week. However, your difficulties might be there 24 hours a day, every day. During our sessions, we will focus on factors which are causing and maintaining your problems, and then look at developing new strategies which could help with these difficulties. What is important is that we develop strategies which work not only in session, but whilst outside of our sessions as well. If the strategies we develop are not useful, then obviously we would need to consider*

Thought to be tested: People in the street laugh at me. *Usual safety behaviour:* Walk fast, look at the ground, avoid looking at people.					
Belief in thought: (0-100%) Before experiment: 90% *After experiment:* 20%					
Experiment to test thought	*Likely problems*	*Strategies to deal with problems*	*Expected outcome*	*Actual outcome*	*Alternative thought*
Look at people in the street when I am walking along, not keep looking down at the floor.	I will not do it properly. I will not do it all because I am not confident enough.	Paul to walk with me on the first occasion, gradually increasing the distance between us. After this try it out for homework.	I will see lots of people laughing and 8/10 people laughing will be directed at me.	Saw a number of people laughing although they appeared not to be laughing at me.	People in the street do laugh although there may be many reasons why this may be the case.

Figure 4.1 Experiment sheet

alternatives. This means that at times it will be helpful if you could undertake tasks outside of our sessions in order to check out if the things we do work in other situations. Do you think that might be useful?

Homework tasks can include assessments in order to identify cognitions or patterns of behaviours, the use of behavioural experiments in order to test out hypotheses, or the adoption of alternative cognitive strategies to accrue data to support or challenge beliefs. Another important homework task is to listen to an audiotape of the session, in order to aid memory and the processing of information.

Common examples of homework tasks include:

- prioritising problem/goal lists
- reviewing formulations
- listening to tapes of therapy sessions
- activity scheduling as a means of developing a baseline of activity collected as part of an assessment
- the data collected from an activity-scheduling assessment can also provide a rationale for change in terms of increasing activity levels and a subsequent behavioural experiment in terms of testing if changes in activity levels can impact on mood
- encouraging people to monitor thoughts through dysfunctional thought records (DTRs)
- testing out the efficacy of safety behaviours through modification or manipulation

A number of people have expressed concern that they feel people may be laughing at them or looking at them whilst they are out in public places. Figure 4.1 shows an experiment designed to test out aspects of safety behaviours, which appeared to be maintaining the problem [this form is based on the behavioural experiment forms developed by Greenberger & Padesky (1995)]. Initially, this had to be undertaken jointly by therapist and client, in order to develop enough confidence to subsequently try this out as a homework task. This is not an uncommon situation.

Time Limited

CT is a time-limited intervention, with the maximum number of sessions generally agreed at the outset of therapy. It can be helpful to break therapy down into blocks of six sessions and at every sixth session review progress to date and contract for a further six if required. Reviewing goals every six sessions should also help them to be SMART. As a guide, the maximum number of sessions is generally around 24–30 and the average is around 12 (for our research study, the maximum number of sessions was 25).

On occasions it has been necessary to have slightly more sessions than 22–30 sessions, although the extra sessions have usually been for case-management or crisis-intervention purposes, rather than additional CT. This is due to the fact that many of the individuals have practical difficulties, and often did not have any other individuals involved with their care.

SUMMARY

It has been argued in Chapter 3 that a psychological intervention with at-risk individuals should be the treatment of choice for this group, as it could specifically target a wide range of problems associated with the prodromal period. The structure and process of CT combine to make it uniquely suitable for preventing transition to psychosis in a way that is acceptable to clients and their carers.

The process of formulation-based CT, with a shared problem and goal list, appears to enhance engagement and enable understanding of the development and maintenance of difficulties. The strategies for change are utilised in the spirit of collaborative empiricism in order to test out hypotheses as opposed to dictating what is required of the individual. The use of homework tasks to underline the strategies discussed in therapy is important to the process, and can validate what takes place during therapy sessions. Finally, the time-limited aspect of therapy allows individuals to feel that they will be able to get on with their lives independently from services and allows an exit strategy, which emphasises the message of hope and recovery.

5

ENGAGEMENT

The practicalities of delivering this type of intervention require some discussion as we have found a number of potential difficulties associated with this kind of work.

Engagement is an important issue when working with any client group, although some groups may be more difficult to engage than others. We have found that if we adhere to certain principles, then it is feasible to effectively engage this client group. However, the at-risk population we are working with are help-seeking and, as such, are interested in accessing some form of treatment for their difficulties (though these are often unrelated to psychosis). Therefore, a problem-orientated approach will be described to facilitate the engagement process, with the development of trust and rapport early on in the therapeutic relationship obviously playing a key role. We feel that this problem-orientated approach is central to negotiating the ethical dilemmas previously discussed, and also to the process of engagement. It is possible that early engagement may lead to future benefits should transition to psychosis occur, including improved adherence with treatment programmes and co-operation with the clinical team. This, in turn, may lead to reduced need for coercive treatment or compulsory admissions to hospital.

PRINCIPLES OF ENGAGEMENT

There are several factors that should be considered when working to engage a client in CT who is considered to be at high risk of future psychosis. The therapist should recognise that the client could be nervous or reluctant to see someone. If the therapist explains this is a common experience, then it can begin to ease tensions, normalise the experience or allow this to be raised and addressed as a problem. The therapist should be aware that psychotic symptoms, even though sub-clinical or fleeting, could well influence communication and information-processing. Therefore, regular feedback, including capsule summaries to check for understanding on behalf of therapist and client, is recommended. This process can also ensure that the client's viewpoint is acknowledged, allowing him/her to feel listened to and understood. Another simple technique to ensure someone feels understood is this: when you ask a question, you should appear interested in the answer – this can be an extremely powerful way of engaging someone in therapy. It might appear a very obvious thing to do, although all too frequently people go through the motions, asking a set routine of questions with little regard for the responses. A client involved with our study commented on his consultations with his GP, who did not look up from his computer when he was discussing symptoms of paranoia and appeared quite disinterested, although he went through the motions of doing a brief assessment. This significantly affected his perceptions of his GP as someone who was not interested in him or his problems.

- Try to identify any common ground between the client and therapist. This can be potentially quite challenging, especially when there are significant differences between the ages and lifestyles of client and therapist. However, if some element of shared experiences can be elicited then this can play a significant role in the engagement process. The therapist should be careful not to spend too much time on this issue if no common ground is forthcoming. Do not fall into the trap of pretending to be interested or know about things about youth culture when this is not the case as this can be seen as patronising and you will be easily caught out.
- Use everyday language that will be understood and avoid jargon and unnecessary technical terminology.
- Ensure that contemporary points of reference are utilised in discussion rather than ones that relate solely to the therapist's world.
- Carefully explain any issues associated with the therapy including the practical aspects of where therapy will take place, the number of sessions and assessment criteria.
- Gather information gradually – do not go at a pace that the client clearly finds difficult.
- Be helpful, active and flexible within the session and do not stick to rigid formats. Be opportunistic if things arise that may be useful therapeutically. The attainment of an early success experience can prove invaluable and is generally recognised within CT as a significant motivating factor.
- Consider the individual's first experience of psychosis and the potential fear that this may well have on the individual with associated thoughts of 'losing control' or 'going mad' and how this may influence their view of therapy and contact with services.
- Be aware of the potential range of reactions to psychotic symptoms and the influence that this may have on their current circumstances, their personality development and their coping skills.
- Consider the social or cultural background of the client and how this may impact on the practical aspects of therapy (such as language barriers, times of day that appointments are set or gender-specific requests). Sociocultural background may also impact on the details of therapy including the fact that psychotic symptoms may well be culture-syntonic, which would require an effort on the part of the therapist to go away and understand some of these issues (and discussion in supervision).

- Recognise the client's and/or carer's attitudes towards services, including previous contacts or stories they may have heard, and how this may impact upon the therapeutic relationship.
- Finally, it is important to appreciate the potential impact overall that even subclinical or fleeting psychotic symptoms could have upon the individual's life.

CASE EXAMPLE

Dennis, a young man, was initially seen by his GP, who then referred him to the primary care psychological therapy service. They referred Dennis on to long-term psychotherapy and he was subsequently referred to our project from there. He was considered hard to engage by the primary care psychologist and it had been suggested that his problems did not fit a brief treatment approach, which that service adopts. The psychotherapy service felt that Dennis's problems were more in line with a developing psychosis, hence their referral to our team. He expressed his main problems as feeling depressed and experiencing panic attacks, although he was also fearful of 'going crazy'. It transpired that his maternal grandmother had a diagnosis of schizophrenia and he was experiencing what he considered to be 'odd ideas'. His grandmother had lived with his family for a number of years and from his accounts it sounded as though she was quite psychotic and her behaviours were the cause of many arguments and difficulties within the family.

Dennis was seen at his GP surgery and during one of the initial sessions he explained that he felt a little nauseous. He was offered a drink of water, which required the therapist to leave the room. On returning with the water Dennis appeared somewhat more anxious than before. Changes in affect are a focus of CT and in-session changes can be very useful in therapy. It transpired that Dennis's main thought had been that the therapist would return with other people who would then transport him by force to the local psychiatric hospital. He had subsequently thought about leaving the room before this could happen to him. Clearly, these thoughts would lead to feelings of anxiety and his desire to run away in the context of these thoughts would have made a great deal of sense. This allowed a cognitive model to be developed highlighting alternative interpretations of the event that would lead to different feelings and behaviours. Dennis's original interpretation made sense in terms of his previous experiences, although it could have had a catastrophic effect on his engagement with the team and services if unidentified.

The dialogue at this point in the session was as follows:

THERAPIST: Hi, here is your drink. You look concerned, has anything happened?
DENNIS: No, nothing, I just got a bit anxious whilst you were out, that's all.
THERAPIST: Would it be possible for you to tell me what was going through your mind when you started to become anxious?
DENNIS: It's nothing really, it seems pretty stupid now.

THERAPIST: I suppose that it may feel stupid now but you seemed quite worried when
                     I first returned. It can be helpful to look at what happened and what was
                     going through your mind when you were concerned.
DENNIS: Well, I started to think that you were going to come back with a load of
                     people and you were going to take me off to some mental hospital and
                     I started to get really worried.
THERAPIST: Well, I think if I had experienced that thought I would have become
                     worried too. Could we spend a little time understanding what has just
                     happened in a bit more detail?
DENNIS: Okay then.

The following cycles of event, thoughts, feelings and behaviours were then collaboratively generated using guided discovery (see Figure 5.1):

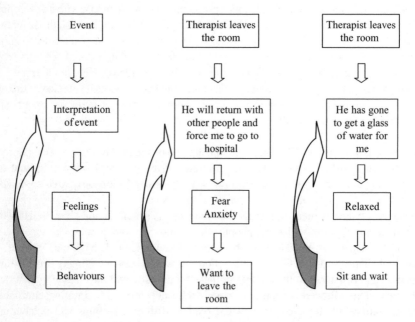

Figure 5.1   Formulation indicating event, belief about event, feelings and behaviours

COLLABORATION

The venue for the sessions should be carefully considered and secondary service settings associated with mental health care should be avoided at all costs. The individual
can (and frequently does) interpret this as another indication of their impending madness, which can serve to increase conviction in unhelpful beliefs and can also lead to

non-attendance at appointments. Providing appointments in settings that are amenable to the client is extremely important – this could be GP surgeries; health centres; youth centres; local community centres or domiciliary visits. It is preferable for sessions to take place at some type of service setting (rather than the client's home) as this can reduce the risk of interruptions from ringing phones, the television or friends coming round, although this has to be balanced against whether the person would attend a service setting at all. If the person will not attend a service setting then domiciliary visits should be provided although safety should always be prioritised and managed. The reasons for non-attendance at service settings should be assessed, as it may be that the individual has significant social anxiety or suspiciousness and a goal of treatment may be the ability to attend sessions at the service setting.

The timing of the session is important and should also be negotiated along with the venue. We have found that a significant proportion of this client group are engaged in some activity such as college or work and do not wish to take time off from this activity to attend an appointment. This means that provision has to be made for clients who are unable to be seen within general 9–5 working hours. It is worth noting that requests for evening appointments are much more common than for early morning appointments, which is unsurprising given the age range of our clients. The ability to reflect this within the service is therefore an important consideration.

At times, it has been important to incorporate case-management and also crisis-intervention strategies. Many people with established psychotic disorders have access to case managers or support workers and some have access to out-of-hours services. However, the high-risk group will have no extra resources to assist them with difficulties they may be facing. Due to this, it can be extremely important to assist with some of the practical problems clients may be facing, such as contacting housing agencies or assisting with benefits. There have also been occasions when crises have occurred and it has been vital to respond to them.

Finally, with this population we have found that sessions can frequently be cancelled due to a range of issues from physical ill health to being too busy with friends. This requires the therapist to be tolerant of this and to continue to offer appointments beyond what would frequently be acceptable in primary care settings.

DIFFICULTIES IN ENGAGEMENT

As described earlier, adhering to certain principles can ease the process of engagement. However, some clients are clearly harder to engage than others. One group of referrals comes from secondary services, which may perceive that the individual requires further monitoring or intervention, although this may not be something the client wants to consider. It is with this group (those who are not themselves directly seeking help) that additional engagement strategies can be required. This may require the therapist to utilise assertive outreach and case-management strategies in order to engage the individual prior to the commencement of CT.

In our experience, it has been necessary, at times, to engage in many activities in order for the individual to trust the therapist and commence working at a cognitive level. Attending court with people, assisting with housing or attending appointments with the police have all been undertaken in an attempt to gain trust and rapport with the individual prior to starting the therapy process. This can seem alien to many cognitive therapists, although people working within an assertive outreach framework will recognise the importance of these activities. It should be noted that, if someone has clear and pressing social needs, such as problems with housing or finance, then these must be addressed; for example, it is unlikely that someone will benefit from CT if they are homeless, and they will certainly struggle to complete their homework.

Another strategy that has been recently employed by our team is to make use of former clients who can be contacted in order to provide a 'reference' for the therapist. If information is provided by someone external to the service, and by someone who can understand what they are experiencing, then this can be an important method of ensuring that the client feels they can trust their therapist.

It has also been necessary to understand any previous contact with services and acknowledge how this may prevent them from wanting to engage with anyone. Giving information that highlights the non-medical interventions employed, alongside enforcing the fact that all interventions are collaborative, has been extremely important. Clearly, this is then backed up by the actions of our team.

These strategies can be extremely effective in engaging individuals who may not initially wish to engage with services, although once this process has begun it can be quite hard to move from a case-management style of interventions to a structured cognitive approach. In view of this, it can be extremely helpful to inform the individual at the start that you are quite happy to assist with any number of practical difficulties, although at some point moving towards a more structured approach to therapy would be advantageous. Other methods of overcoming this problem may include another member of the team providing case management, although there is the possibility that the client may well end up engaging with this person rather than the therapist. One way round this may be for both a therapist and another member of the team to make themselves available for practical issues when starting to engage with the individual. As the client becomes more engaged with the team, the therapist can gradually move towards providing a more structured cognitive approach. Alternatively, if other team members are not available, then the therapist can have separate sessions where one is the focus for cognitive and behavioural interventions, and the next has a more general approach. At times, however, this can prove difficult for both therapist and client to sustain.

SUMMARY

In this chapter some of the practical difficulties of working with this client group are discussed. The importance of engagement is emphasised throughout this chapter and several strategies for overcoming difficulties with this process have been suggested. These include practical suggestions such as the location and timing of therapy sessions and also strategies which can be explored in session to examine beliefs that may inhibit engagement. Some beliefs may be based on clients' own direct experience of services as many services have a range of quite intrusive interventions. However, their beliefs could be as a result of media perceptions of 'madness' and the portrayal of what this entails. Taking time to understand and formulate what may be affecting the engagement process is extremely important.

Finally, we have outlined how it may be necessary to undertake more supportive case-management-based interventions in an effort to develop trust and rapport with an individual, prior to commencing CT. However, this strategy can also involve difficulties, and these were reviewed with recommendations for overcoming them.

6

THEORY, ASSESSMENT AND FORMULATION

A COGNITIVE MODEL DESCRIBING THE ONSET OF PSYCHOSIS

Recent psychological models of psychosis have tended to focus on symptoms rather than psychiatric syndromes, as has been advocated by Bentall (1990). There are various examples of these models (Bentall, Kinderman & Kaney, 1994; Chadwick & Birchwood, 1994; Morrison, 1998a; Morrison, Haddock & Tarrier, 1995), which have helped to understand the maintenance of specific symptoms (such as hallucinations and delusions) and subsequently guide clinical interventions. However, most of these models have had little to say about the development of psychosis. Clients in a high-risk population may not have experienced well-formed or fully fledged psychotic symptoms. One of the guiding principles of CT is that the disorder being treated should have a cognitive model that explains the onset and maintenance of symptoms and guides the treatment of these symptoms, so a model that can be applied with individuals at risk of psychosis is required.

Recently there have been models (Garety et al., 2001; Morrison, 2001) developed which enable us to conceptualise the onset and development of psychotic symptoms. The model developed by Morrison (2001) focuses upon the interpretation of intrusions and specifically implicates the cultural unacceptability of the interpretation of the intrusion in determining whether someone is deemed to be psychotic. The model (see Figure 6.1) suggests that similar processes are involved in the development of psychotic and non-psychotic disorders. Wells and Matthews's (1994) S-REF (self-regulatory executive function) model of emotional dysfunction specifically implicates faulty self and social knowledge, including metacognition (thinking about thinking) and declarative and procedural beliefs.

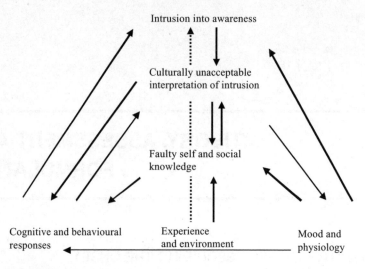

Intrusion into awareness

Culturally unacceptable
interpretation of intrusion

Faulty self and social
knowledge

Cognitive and behavioural
responses

Experience
and environment

Mood and
physiology

Figure 6.1   Morrison's model of psychosis
Source: from Morrison (2001)

Declarative beliefs are statements about the self, world and others, such as 'I am bad' or 'Others are dangerous', whereas *procedural beliefs* are like rules for guiding the selection of information-processing strategies (such as 'being paranoid helps to avoid being hurt'). Initial onset of psychotic symptoms often seems to be related to an inability to generate alternative (culturally acceptable) explanations for internal or external events. This may be due to a lack of trusting or supportive social relationships that would facilitate the normalisation of such interpretations (French et al., 2001). The lack of such relationships is likely to contribute to the failure to correct faulty self and social knowledge [this may help to explain the short-term benefits derived from befriending interventions (Sensky et al., 2000)]. The model also implicates unhelpful cognitive responses (such as selective attention and dysfunctional thought-control strategies) and behavioural responses (such as safety behaviours and avoidance) in the maintenance of distress and psychotic interpretations. As this model integrates many of the elements that have been identified in the development and maintenance of non-psychotic disorders, such as panic, obsessions, social phobia and depression, it is easily adapted to address both psychotic and non-psychotic concerns. This makes it especially suitable for a heterogeneous high-risk population, some of whom have psychotic experiences and prioritise these as a problem, some of whom have psychotic experiences but prioritise other problems, and some of whom have no psychotic experiences but may be concerned about developing psychosis because of a family history.

Our interventions are based on idiosyncratic case formulations derived from this model, incorporating clients' life experiences, current environment, self and social knowledge, intrusions and their interpretations of intrusions, and their emotional, behavioural, cognitive and physiological responses. This also facilitates the use of specific models of emotional disorders (e.g. Clark, 1999; Salkovskis, 1996; Wells & Matthews, 1994), from which these concepts were adopted, when relevant.

ASSESSMENT

The process of assessment is designed to provide information that will assist with the collaborative development of a shared formulation that describes the client's difficulties in a way that is testable and can be translated into strategies for change. Therefore, the model can guide the topics to be covered in an assessment.

Conducting Interviews

The major focus of a cognitive-behavioural assessment is the verbal interview that examines people's presenting problems in terms of the five systems (cognitive, behavioural, emotional, physiological and environmental). Cognitive components include what a person thinks and believes (including thoughts about their psychotic experiences), images that they have, what they pay attention to, how they pay attention, whether there are any information-processing biases involved, what they remember and how they control unwanted thoughts. Behavioural components include what they do before, during and after a difficult situation, whether there are any safety behaviours designed to avert feared outcomes and whether they avoid certain things or places. Affective components include how a person feels emotionally before, during and after a situation and physiological components include how a person responds physically, their sleep patterns and any organic factors. The environmental components include housing, cultural milieu, family or housemates, friends and opportunities for meaningful and valued activities. Assessment should examine each area in detail, and can begin to overlap with formulation by looking for thought–emotion–behaviour cycles (thus helping to develop a maintenance formulation for specific difficulties or situations). This will also aid socialisation to the cognitive model.

QUESTIONS TO HELP ASSESS COGNITIVE COMPONENTS INCLUDE:

- What was going through your mind at the time?
- What was the first thing that you thought?
- Did anything trigger the way you were feeling?
- Did you have an image of the event in your mind? What did it look like?

These questions can be particularly helpful when used in conjunction with affect shifts or real-life situations.

The model suggests that intrusions are often interpreted in a manner that can increase the distress associated with them or their frequency. Questions that can assess such metacognitive interpretations include:

- What did having that thought mean to you?
- Could anything happen as a result of having such a thought?
- Is it normal/okay/acceptable to have such thoughts? If not, why not?
- What would happen if you could not stop these thoughts?
- Does having such thoughts say anything about you?
- Are there any disadvantages or advantages to having such thoughts?

Such questions can be applied to intrusive thoughts, negative automatic thoughts, paranoid thoughts, angry thoughts, etc.

It is also important to assess what attentional factors may be implicated using questions such as:

- When you were in that situation, what were you (most) aware of?
- What did you notice first?
- Were you on the look-out for such thoughts/feelings/behaviours?
- When you felt scared/sad/angry, what were you most conscious of?
- How do you think you seemed to other people?
- Once you noticed that, were you able to focus on anything else?

It is often important to assess safety-seeking behaviours that clients use to prevent a feared outcome from occurring (see Salkovskis, 1996). Once identified, such behaviours can be manipulated to test hypotheses and facilitate disconfirmation of beliefs or interpretations of intrusions. Safety behaviours can be identified using questions such as:

- When you thought that this was happening/going to happen, what did you do to prevent it?
- If you had not done this, what would have happened?
- Is there anything you do to control your symptom?
- Do you do anything to help you cope or to hide the difficulty?

Avoidance can be conceptualised as an extreme form of safety behaviour and assessed using similar questions such as:

- Is there anything that you avoid doing because of this problem?
- Do you ever try to escape from this situation?
- Does this difficulty stop you from going anywhere?

Safety behaviours are discussed in more detail in Chapter 9, including assessment and treatment strategies.

Emotional responses should be assessed and rated for intensity in relation to individual situations, idiosyncratic thoughts and behaviours. When eliciting and rating emotions it is important to use the client's own language, and to ask for clarification to check that we share the understanding of such labels. Physical responses to individual situations, idiosyncratic thoughts, emotions and behaviours should also be assessed and particular attention should be given to dissociative experiences and anxiety sensations (such as palpitations, dizziness, blurred vision, tension, breathlessness, sweating, trembling or shaking, butterflies in the stomach and difficulty swallowing). This can be done using questions such as:

- Did you notice any physical changes in response to that?
- When in that situation, what was happening to your body?
- When you were thinking that, how did you feel physically?
- Was there a physical feeling that made you believe that this was really happening?

Historical Factors

In addition to the here-and-now focus of CT, it is important to have a historical context in which to base any analysis of current difficulties. Eliciting information regarding a client's early life experiences and the beliefs that they have developed as a result of these can do this. Assessment should cover the following areas of developmental history:

- Overall impression of childhood
- Family history (siblings, parents, any separations)
- Happiest memories
- Worst memories
- School
- Friendships
- Sexual history
- Cultural/religious history
- Any uncomfortable sexual experiences
- Any physical violence
- Current environment (accommodation, finances, activities, employment/education, culture)
- Relevant historical factors for specific symptoms (e.g. if paranoia is an issue, asking about drug use, personal safety considerations such as living in an area of high street crime, contact with police and prison services)

Beliefs

The assessment should also cover the beliefs that people have formed about themselves, the world, other people and their future as a result of these experiences. The rules for living that people develop to accommodate these beliefs should also be assessed (e.g. if a client believes that they are worthless, they may develop a rule, based on interactions with parents with high expectations, that 'If I am not perfect, then I am worthless'. Assessment should also include the compensatory behavioural strategies that they develop to try to follow these rules (e.g. never saying no to things and striving for perfection).

Below are some examples of some core beliefs and corresponding compensatory beliefs.

Core belief	People cannot be trusted.
Compensatory belief	If I let my guard down I will get hurt.
Core belief	I am a disappointment to everyone.
Compensatory belief	If I get to know someone they may find out I am a disappointment.
Core belief	I am weird and must not let people see.
Compensatory belief	If I get to know people they will find out I am weird.
Core belief	I have no place in the world.
Compensatory belief	I should be perfect to fit in.
Core belief	I am a bad person.
Compensatory belief	When things go wrong I am to blame.

Drug Use

The assessment process should also include an analysis of drug use. Frequently, drug use is perceived as causative of psychosis, which in some instances may be the case. However, at other times the taking of drugs may be an attempt at self-medication as a means of managing distress associated with beliefs. Therefore, careful analysis needs to be undertaken not only in terms of the range of drugs being taken, their quantity and frequency, but also the context in which they are being taken. A medication history should be taken including current and past medications; this should also take into account an assessment of any potential side effects experienced through the taking of these medications. It can be helpful to assess whether the individual takes their medication as prescribed or whether they self-medicate using an alternative strategy.

Risk

Finally, risk should be assessed in relation to self and others. The Beck Hopelessness Scale is a useful means of detecting potential suicidal ideation. If this is detected then a standard assessment of suicidal intent should be undertaken. Many areas have their own risk assessment procedures, which should be followed. In terms of risk to others, if this is indicated it should again be assessed following standard procedures.

FORMULATION

The inclusion of formulation-driven interventions can be seen as one of the main differences between CT and merely using cognitive techniques. Formulation-driven interventions are considered to be central to the process of CT.

When treating certain disorders (e.g. panic disorder) it can be feasible and is recommended (Wells, 1997) that at the end of the first contact a preliminary formulation is devised to explain symptomatology. However, for this client group it is envisaged that this may prove too ambitious, and it is suggested that a preliminary formulation is devised by the second session. This is then enhanced throughout the rest of the therapy process, with new material added as therapy continues. The development of a comprehensive formulation could be viewed as potentially threatening towards the engagement process and if the therapist is insensitive to the client's needs, then this may well be the case. However, if the client is shown that the formulation is a useful way for the therapist to understand their problems, but also a guide to tackling them, then the process of formulation can, in itself, enhance engagement and reflects a central theme of CT, which is collaborative empiricism.

Initially, formulation should be done slowly in order to ensure that the client understands, and is in agreement with, it; this is probably done most effectively using vicious circles incorporating recent specific incidents to illustrate the maintenance of particularly problematic symptoms or situations, as identified in the problem list. Such a formulation can be based on heuristic models of the links between cognitive, behavioural, emotional and physiological factors; these can either be generic (e.g. Greenberger & Padesky, 1995) or in relation to specific psychotic symptoms (Chadwick, Birchwood & Trower, 1996; Morrison, 1998b). For instance, the approach to auditory hallucinations outlined by Morrison (1998a) is easily modified to provide a maintenance formulation illustrating factors involved in a client's idiosyncratic experience of hearing voices.

The cognitive formulation of a client's difficulties should be used as an alternative explanation of symptoms, along with all others that can be generated by the client (in collaboration with the therapist) including that the symptoms can be based in reality. This will help to engage and socialise a client to a cognitive way of working, and will facilitate the choice of intervention strategies and homework tasks. Once a formulation is obtained, verbal and behavioural reattribution methods can then be used to reach some conclusion about which explanation best accounts for the client's experiences.

The choice of strategies used for intervention should be determined by the idiosyncratic formulation, and often be negotiated through discussion with the client. The aim of intervention is to reduce distress and disability and to increase quality of life. Keeping these aims in mind, the selection and prioritisation of clients' goals from a

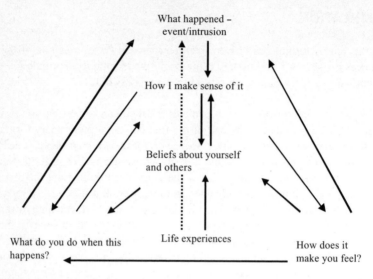

Figure 6.2 Client-friendly version of Morrison's model of psychosis

problem list will also guide intervention (it is important to begin with the problem that is most amenable to change in order to provide a success experience in therapy). There are obviously many similarities between working with clients at risk of psychosis and those with other disorders (for instance, if a client's goals are to have a more active social life, to have a tidier flat or to feel less anxious when getting on a bus, then these problems would be addressed in the same way as for a client who is not at risk, although the formulation could be used to predict certain difficulties that may occur when implementing such interventions).

The formulation based on the model is typically developed within the first two sessions. The aim is to move from general, abstract concerns the person may have to more specific ways of understanding them. One aim of this process is also to highlight occasions when their interpretations do not lead to distress. It can be helpful to utilise the client's own language within the formulation rather than intrusions into awareness and a typical format for a client-friendly formulation is presented in Figure 6.2.

An example of a detailed idiosyncratic formulation is given in Figure 6.3.

SUMMARY

As advocated by Bentall (1990), recent psychological models of psychosis have tended to focus on symptoms rather than psychiatric syndromes. CT should follow a psychological model of the disorder being treated that explains the onset and maintenance of symptoms and guides the treatment of these symptoms.

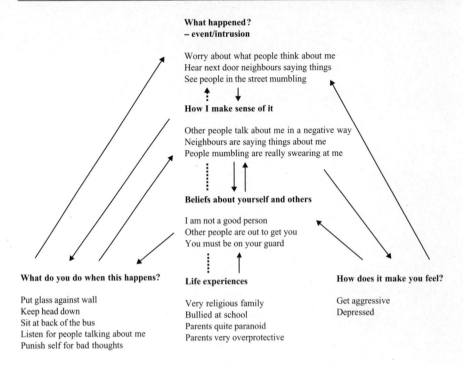

What happened?
– event/intrusion

Worry about what people think about me
Hear next door neighbours saying things
See people in the street mumbling

How I make sense of it

Other people talk about me in a negative way
Neighbours are saying things about me
People mumbling are really swearing at me

Beliefs about yourself and others

I am not a good person
Other people are out to get you
You must be on your guard

What do you do when this happens?

Put glass against wall
Keep head down
Sit at back of the bus
Listen for people talking about me
Punish self for bad thoughts

Life experiences

Very religious family
Bullied at school
Parents quite paranoid
Parents very overprotective

How does it make you feel?

Get aggressive
Depressed

Figure 6.3   Idiosyncratic version of Morrison's model of psychosis

In setting the scene for Chapter 7 on normalisation, the model described in this chapter suggests that similar processes are involved in the development of psychotic and non-psychotic disorders. The model also implicates unhelpful cognitive and behavioural responses in the maintenance of distress and psychotic interpretations. This makes it especially suitable for a heterogeneous high-risk population, with varying symptom problems and symptoms, and interventions are based on idiosyncratic case formulations derived from this model.

The cognitive-behavioural assessment should overlap with formulation by looking for thought–emotion–behaviour cycles that can aid socialisation to the cognitive model. Throughout the chapter, questions are provided which can assist this process. The formulation should be derived early on in therapy as a means of directing therapy, since formulation-driven interventions are considered to be central to the process of CT. The cognitive formulation of a client's difficulties should be used as an alternative explanation of symptoms, along with all others that can be generated by the client including that the symptoms could be based in reality. The importance of safety behaviours, core beliefs and their corresponding compensatory beliefs are also emphasised throughout the chapter and examples are provided.

PART III

CHANGE STRATEGIES

7

NORMALISATION

WHY SHOULD WE NORMALISE PSYCHOTIC SYMPTOMS?

In this chapter, we discuss the importance of normalising psychotic experiences. This approach to existing psychotic symptoms has been extensively utilised by Kingdon and Turkington (1994). This is consistent with Strauss's (1969) hypothesis that psychotic phenomena lie on a continuum with normal processes. Consistent with this viewpoint, epidemiological studies suggest a higher incidence of psychotic phenomena in the general population than is to be expected from studies of psychiatric admissions. For example, approximately 5% of the population experience auditory hallucinations (Tien, 1991; van Os et al., 2000) and about 9% hold delusional beliefs (van Os et al., 2000). There is also evidence that psychotic phenomena can be detected in apparently mentally healthy primary care clients by means of self-report questionnaires. For example, Verdoux et al. (1998) found that 16% of a large sample (n = 462) of primary care patients experienced verbal hallucinations and 26% endorsed believing there to be a conspiracy against them. The work of Grimby (1993) examined people who lost their partner after they had been together for a long period of time. In this work, Grimby found that it was extremely common for the bereaved individual to hear or see their partner following their death. In such cases, we do not assume that such experiences should be medicated or pathologised. Instead, we would talk to the bereaved individual about the experience, explaining that this is frequently a part of the grieving process, and in many cases how comforting this may be. In our personal and professional lives, if we were presented with this scenario, then it would be highly unlikely that we would come to the conclusion that this individual was on the brink of madness. Why, then, do we jump to this exact conclusion when similar experiences are found in younger people despite the fact that the majority of these experiences can also be just as easily understood and normalised if we take time to understand their context? In the case of the bereaved individual the context is highly visible, and clear links between the experience and recent events are easily made. This makes it easy for us to understand. If, however, the context is not as accessible and it is hard to understand why someone is starting to have strange experiences, then we are more likely to conceptualise this as psychosis. The strategy discussed throughout this book is that taking time to understand context, and making links between the context and the experience, can help normalise experiences for the individual and others and provide a functional alternative explanation for such experiences.

Since the introduction of the normalising approach (see Kingdon & Turkington, 1994), many therapists have adopted this strategy as a means of making sense of what was previously conceived as bizarre and incomprehensible. However, normalisation does not solely relate to how the therapist makes sense of the information, but also includes how they behave in the face of such information. Frequently, clinicians faced with an individual who appears at risk of developing psychosis will have fears and concerns about the individual, about how they should be managed and about the course of psychosis. The individual may well be extremely concerned about disclosing symptoms (see Chapter 12), and if the first person they discuss them with explains that they should accompany them to a casualty department, see a psychiatrist and/or take some medication, then this will clearly reinforce their belief that they are 'going mad'. An important message for clinicians is not to panic. It can be seen from the work examining relapse in psychosis (Gumley & Power, 2000) that catastrophic fears regarding impending relapse can accelerate the process of relapse. A similar process can be observed in the development of an initial episode of psychosis. Drawing on the previous chapter, we can see that psychotic symptoms can be conceptualised as part of normal experience and understood using normal psychological processes. If this is the case, then adopting a psychological, formulation-based approach should impact upon the problems faced by individuals at high risk of developing psychosis. Therefore, in this chapter, strategies to manage the process of normalisation with this client group will be considered.

However, prior to any change strategies being utilised, it is important to consider the role of any such beliefs as many can have some benefits to them. A simple strategy to employ is to check out the advantages and disadvantages of holding a belief. This can then be used by the client and therapist to collaboratively agree on whether change strategies should be implemented. A common example of this is where an individual is suspicious of others. Their suspicion typically will have arisen out of their life experiences (e.g. being bullied). Clearly, being suspicious of others if you are being bullied can have some protective factor in that it may minimise the potential for further bullying. Therefore, an individual may wish to maintain some element of suspicion, which in today's society is not a bad thing. However, the individual may wish to extend their ability to trust others and be able to reduce levels of distress so the belief may need modifying in some way; this can be achieved in accordance with their wishes if the therapist is aware of the pros and cons of this belief. Therefore, the process of assessing advantages/disadvantages of a belief should be undertaken before any belief modification is commenced.

DON'T PANIC: CLINICIAN'S MESSAGE

As mentioned, this is an important message for clinicians working in this area. One of the main reasons that clinicians panic when faced with an individual who is beginning to present with symptoms of psychosis is due to their preconceptions about the diagnosis of schizophrenia. The connotations associated with this diagnosis are heavily laden with doom and despair. Schizophrenia has been conceptualised for many years as consistent with the Kraepelinian view, which assumes that schizophrenia is a biological disorder that has an inevitably deteriorating course. If this Kraepelinian view is held, then it will undoubtedly lead to beliefs on behalf of the clinician that the most effective way to assist the individual is through a biological mechanism (if anything at all can stop or delay the deterioration). This will generally require the person to see a psychiatrist, who will usually be based in a psychiatric hospital or community mental health centre, and this will confirm the individual's beliefs that they are 'going mad', as they themselves suspected. However, many people are now challenging this view and, in order to move away from the concept of schizophrenia, are utilising the concept of psychotic or unusual experiences instead:

> Traditionally, psychotic experiences have been thought of as symptoms of 'mental illness' such as schizophrenia or manic depression, and the people who experience them have been referred to as 'patients' or 'sufferers'. More recently it has been suggested that there are other ways of thinking about these experiences, and that, therefore, medical terms are not always the only or best ones to use.

> We have avoided pejorative terms such as schizophrenics. Not only do such terms assume the undisputed existence of physical illness, but in our view they also portray people as less than human.
>
> (Kinderman & Cooke, 2000; p. 10)

As previously discussed, this is important when dealing with early psychosis, and encourages a more symptom-orientated management approach. Supervision is an important factor in maintaining a hopeful outlook and keeping an open mind.

DON'T PANIC: CLIENT'S MESSAGE

Most people have some experience of schizophrenia, even if this is via the media. Many people will have personal experiences of schizophrenia, whether through family or friends, and the treatment associated with it frequently means the prescription of medication and admission to hospital. If someone's only perspective of schizophrenia comes from the media, then this can be even worse, as it is extremely rare that the media portray a positive view of schizophrenia. When we consider the images from the media regarding schizophrenia, they are likely to include films such as *One Flew Over the Cuckoo's Nest* or news reports of people with schizophrenia committing murder or other acts of aggression (whether to themselves or others). It has been pointed out that there are very few positive or successful recovery stories available, with which people with psychosis could challenge such hopeless and pessimistic views (May, 2000). Therefore, these experiences will inform people's expectations of what may happen to them, which would sensibly evoke fear and anxiety, which in turn can then evoke further symptoms, setting up a vicious circle. Also, if a clinician encourages biological treatment through psychiatry, then it can also lead to the individual being very concerned about disclosing their symptoms again. Indeed, the development of negative symptoms, such as flat or blunted affect or poverty of speech, may be a mechanism (or safety behaviour) for avoiding feared outcomes such as increases in medication or admission to hospital (Morrison et al., 2003).

Many people who meet criteria for being at high risk have expressed concern over their experiences and have felt that they are at the point of impending madness. This has usually led clinicians to become fearful and encourage swift psychiatric intervention. However, this action may exacerbate the very symptoms they are attempting to resolve.

CASE EXAMPLE (1)

Joe is a young man who was seen by a counsellor who was concerned about his mental state. He was experiencing the onset of psychotic symptoms including visual and auditory hallucinations. He was extremely concerned about these experiences and had thoughts of self-harm as a consequence. It had taken an enormous amount of effort for Joe to be able to enter the counselling department and, subsequently, disclose his concerns. The counsellor was extremely concerned and encouraged him to attend the local casualty department for psychiatric assessment. He refused to do this because of his concerns that he may be perceived as 'mad' and that this would lead to him being admitted to hospital (which may well have been accurate). He did, however, agree to meeting up with a member of our team. This was because we were happy to meet him at a neutral venue, we agreed not to involve his GP unless there were concerns about safety, and it was made clear that we were not involved in prescribing medication or admitting people to hospital. Despite this, Joe was still extremely anxious about meeting someone from the team and spent some time outside the department deliberating about whether to attend or not. Notwithstanding his concerns, he managed to attend an appointment for assessment.

CLIENT: What is it that you do?
THERAPIST: I work with people who may be developing certain kinds of mental health problems. We ask a range of questions in order to see if you are potentially at risk and if you were we would try to offer some help regarding your concerns.
CLIENT: What do you mean certain kinds of mental health problems?
THERAPIST: Well, I work with people who may be at risk of developing problems that could be described as psychosis. This means that they may be

starting to experience some unusual thoughts or hearing odd things or starting to worry that people may be saying things about them. If you are considered to be at risk this does not mean that you will definitely become psychotic. It is only the minority of the people we see who would go on to develop this problem.

CLIENT: So things may just go away by themselves?

THERAPIST: It is entirely possible that things may well resolve themselves and go away and for most people that is what happens. However, another possibility is that things could get worse over a period of time. What we would like to do is tackle these things at this point rather than just leaving them in an effort to resolve them early and also work towards preventing them happening again or minimising the potential for them happening again. I suppose our main aim is to maximise the chance of you being in the group where your symptoms go away.

CLIENT: If I am at risk, then, what would you do to me?

THERAPIST: We use a psychological treatment called cognitive therapy, which looks at the links between how we think, what we feel and how we behave, so we would not be offering you medication or admitting you to hospital. If it became necessary, then that may be something we would have to discuss, but initially we would spend time trying to understand your problems and see if there was a psychological way of managing them.

The person who undertook the assessment was calm, friendly and open and, importantly, their actions were not to encourage Joe to immediately attend casualty or psychiatric services, but to offer a more acceptable alternative. Significantly, he found the questions regarding his psychotic symptoms accurately reflected the experiences he was having and this led him to the assumption that his experiences may, in fact, not be so unusual (since the assessor was asking extremely pertinent questions). The message given from the team, not only verbally, but also behaviourally, indicated that we did not think the person was 'going mad'. He was not encouraged to see a psychiatrist or go for further assessments at casualty and was not offered medication. However, his problems were listened to and taken extremely seriously and he was offered further appointments to explore his concerns in more detail.

THERAPIST: It sounds like you are extremely concerned about these experiences?

CLIENT: I am, and when I tell people they want me to go and see a psychiatrist and that makes me even more concerned. I don't want to end up in hospital.

THERAPIST: From what you have told me, it does not appear that you need to go to hospital. However, I would be extremely keen to see if we could meet up very soon to spend more time trying to understand the experiences you are having and how they affect you. Would that be all right?

CLIENT: I suppose so.

This process can provide a means of decatastrophising symptoms, in contrast to the catastrophic interpretations that can frequently be displayed by primary care teams. The other vital component is to offer assistance with understanding the psychotic experiences, something that may not happen in Community Mental Health Teams (CMHTs). Frequently, due to competing workloads, CMHTs are concerned with individuals with established rather than emerging psychotic symptoms, so prodromal or at-risk clients are often discharged. It is extremely important that the individual feels that they will be supported in managing these distressing experiences and that they will be listened to. Current service provision, which passes individuals from one service to another (often with little assistance offered until things reach crisis point), does very little to build confidence in services and may be another factor affecting future engagement.

NORMALISING INFORMATION AS EDUCATION

As previously discussed, this strategy draws upon the existing body of work described by Kingdon and Turkington (1994). Their strategy allows distress associated with symptoms to be managed by normalising the experience and gives the person access to information about various situations that could lead someone to experience psychotic phenomena. There are several areas that may cause people at risk of psychosis to become distressed, which may be amenable to normalising. These are extremely similar to those found in people with established psychosis. For example, Morrison et al. (2003) suggest that normalising information regarding the triggers for and prevalence of psychotic experiences, intrusive thoughts, the diagnosis of schizophrenia and thought suppression, can be extremely beneficial, if the provision of such information is dictated by the formulation. It can also be useful to provide information about your actions as a therapist. It should be stressed, however, that normalisation is different from minimisation, and the distress associated with such experiences should never be dismissed.

CASE EXAMPLE (2)

Rachel, a 26-year-old woman, was referred by her GP because she felt that people were talking about her. This had arisen after she had begun to experience intrusive thoughts about harming her young child. Rachel felt there was a possibility that people might be able to read her mind and, if this was the case, then they might be able see that she was a bad mother. As a consequence of this she avoided going out and was unable to continue her work as a receptionist. Rachel was assessed by one of our team, entered the study via the attenuated symptom route, and was seen for a total of 12 sessions over a period of five months. The initial session focused upon engagement and assessment. At Rachel's request all sessions took place at her GP's surgery and at times that were convenient and negotiated. This process enabled Rachel to feel that she had some control over, and was contributing to, therapy, thereby enhancing collaboration.

At the initial assessment Rachel was encouraged to describe her problems. She was clearly frightened but was able to disclose that she was having unwanted thoughts about harming her son. Throughout, she was very clear that she had no intention or desire to act on these thoughts; however, she was terrified that, if she thought something then there was a possibility of it happening (thought–action fusion, as described by Rachman, 1993). Also, as previously described, she was concerned that other people may be able to read her thoughts. She also worried that, if this was the case, then people might arrange to have her son taken away from her. In order to avoid this happening, Rachel was increasingly isolating herself, and she was finding it impossible to take her son to the local playgroup. Rachel felt that she must be a bad or evil person because she was unable to control these thoughts. Finally, she was coming to the conclusion that if there was a possibility of her harming her son then he should in fact be taken away from her, an idea which terrified her.

Rachel had not disclosed these fears in such detail to anyone previously. She was extremely concerned that the therapist would act upon what she had said and have her son taken away from her. However, she felt that if she was going to harm her son then she should tell someone before she did so. In CT, it is important to try to achieve an early success experience, principally as this can alleviate distress for the client but it can also give hope and enhance engagement with the therapy process. Rachel was given sufficient time to disclose her symptoms and the therapist was interested in hearing about her thoughts and wanted to understand what was happening. The assessment clearly indicated that her thoughts were intrusive in nature. It was her fear of acting on her thoughts and also the belief that others may read her thoughts that caused her distress. Rachel was initially baffled by the therapist's apparent lack of fear for her son's safety and when this was discussed this was a significant comfort to her. In addition, she was shown the research paper written by Rachman and De Silva (1978), which describes intrusive thoughts and includes many examples of people having unacceptable thoughts about harming loved ones. This served to normalise her thoughts and reduce her distress.

During the session the main intervention chosen was to test the belief Rachel held about the need to control her thoughts. In common with many people with obsessional difficulties, when Rachel experienced a problematic intrusive thought she adopted thought suppression (Salkovskis et al., 1998) in an effort to force it out of her mind. Rachel felt this should be an effective strategy, and therefore agreed to test out how effective it was, clearly discounting any previous data regarding this method of controlling her unwanted thoughts. Rachel was asked not to think of a pink elephant for 30 seconds, as suggested by Salkovskis and Kirk (1989). The resulting picture of a pink elephant immediately springing to mind (the paradoxical effect of thought suppression – see Wegner et al., 1987) served to enable some normalisation of her experiences. It also indicated that her strategy may not be the most effective and, significantly, that it may well increase the intrusions in terms of frequency, duration and intensity. Homework was set which was to listen to the audiotape of the session and also to consider what strategy she adopted when she experienced one of her intrusive thoughts.

In this case, it was the attenuated psychotic symptoms that led Rachel to being referred and suitable for the study. Rachel was gradually developing more and more conviction about the fact that others were talking about her and were capable of reading her mind. Rachel was becoming increasingly depressed and anxious and was unable to see a way out of her predicament. However, within a few sessions, Rachel was able to recognise that there was little evidence to suggest that she was a bad mother. In fact, she had begun to accumulate data to suggest the opposite, that perhaps she was actually a good mother. She found that the intrusions themselves had reduced significantly once she understood the nature of them and had adopted alternative management strategies. The emphasis of the intervention was about normalising her experiences and giving her access to information that supported this, whereas her previous strategies born out of fear had actually prevented this process.

SUMMARY

This chapter emphasises the importance of normalising psychotic experiences. Kingdon and Turkington (1994) have highlighted the importance of this technique for existing psychotic symptoms. Clinicians regularly report concerns about working with an individual who appears at risk of developing psychosis, regarding how they should be managed and about the course of psychosis. Typically, the actions of the clinician can reinforce the beliefs the individual has regarding their own sanity (i.e. they are 'going mad'). However, it is possible to conceptualise psychotic symptoms as a variant of normal experience, which can be understood using normal psychological processes. A symptom-based approach to this group, rather than a diagnostic approach, is most suited to this process. However, what is important is that the distress associated with these symptoms is taken seriously. Normalisation does not just mean telling someone that things are fine, or that if they change some aspect of their life, then their problems will resolve. Allowing the individual to recognise that they are having experiences that are much more common than they (and many clinicians) believe, within a supportive therapeutic relationship, is crucial to the process. Merely telling someone that they are normal and that there is nothing to worry about, according to our client's previous experiences, is of little value in addressing their difficulties.

8

GENERATING AND EVALUATING ALTERNATIVE EXPLANATIONS

INTRODUCTION

As discussed in the previous chapter, psychotic phenomena are a common experience within the general population. These phenomena can be conceptualised as intrusions, as described in the model of psychosis (Morrison, 2001) discussed in Chapter 6. It is the culturally unacceptable interpretation of these intrusions that leads to the intrusion being labelled as psychotic. The interpretation of the intrusion can also influence cognitive, emotional and behavioural responses, and this has been well demonstrated in psychotic populations (Birchwood & Chadwick, 1997; Chadwick & Birchwood, 1994; Morrison & Baker, 2000).

In the early stages of psychosis, explanations of anomalous experiences may not have been fully explored by the client. However, Moller and Husby's (2000) research suggests that fear and preoccupation with intrusions is central to the development of psychosis. Some individuals are uncertain about the nature of their experiences. They may have considered a range of possibilities, but this is usually without an evaluative framework underlying this process. The ability to generate a range of possibilities and then evaluate the evidence for each of them in a structured manner is the main focus of this chapter. Clearly this is not a technique only used with this client group, and has been described by therapists working with many different disorders (e.g. Beck et al., 1979; Greenberger & Padesky, 1995; Wells, 1997). However, as we have indicated, we believe that many of the processes in the high-risk group are similar to those experienced in other emotional disorders.

Examining the form and content of intrusions is extremely important. If they are thoughts, then the content of the thoughts should be assessed, as should the idiosyncratic meaning of having such thoughts. If they are images, then the content of the imagery should be assessed in detail, as should the meaning that is encapsulated within such images. Typically, with intrusive thoughts, suppression is utilised as a coping strategy and demonstrating the rebound effect associated with this coping strategy can be useful. This can be achieved through experiments such as asking someone to deliberately not think of a target thought, as described in the case example in Chapter 7.

As with clients who have established psychotic or anxiety symptoms, generating possible explanations for the experience can be extremely useful in reducing distress and helping people evaluate the accuracy of their initial interpretations. As with many elements of CT, learning the process of this intervention is important, in addition to the specific examples that are dealt with in sessions. Clearly, the content of the alternative explanations generated requires some attention and is the subject of evaluation but, as with all aspects of CT, it is the skill-acquisition that is most important. The aim is to assist with generating alternative explanations that are less distressing and more consistent with evidence gathered. It is also important to evaluate the advantages and disadvantages of a particular interpretation or strategy prior to generating alternatives and examining evidence, since it may be functional for the person at that particular time, or it may first be necessary to provide a different way of achieving the benefits.

A common explanation for intrusions, which is frequently reported by our clients, is that they believe they are in some way losing control or 'going mad'. Unfortunately, it is this belief that leads to reluctance to check out interpretations with others (see Chapter 12). Frequently, clients believe that if other people knew what they were thinking, then this could lead to them being admitted to hospital, which in some cases could be a true reflection of the systems currently in place. This means that the therapist must work hard to establish trust in order for the client to feel comfortable expressing their fears. It is important in therapy to identify occasions when these thoughts may be active. A case example of this is provided in Chapter 5. Carefully designed behavioural experiments can be utilised in order to evaluate catastrophic predictions of what would happen if psychotic symptoms were to be disclosed.

The development of an exhaustive list of explanations is essential, and time should be taken to ensure all possibilities are included. The therapist should utilise Socratic dialogue in order to assist the client in developing a comprehensive list of possibilities for their intrusions. Once this list has been established, belief ratings for each of the alternatives should be obtained, and ratings between 0 and 100 (i.e. %) give sufficient sensitivity to measure changes in conviction. Where they fit on the scale should obviously be left up to the client, although anchor points should be agreed between client and therapist (such as 0 = *do not believe this at all*, and 100 = *believe it to be completely true, with no doubt at all*).

Example

THERAPIST: Sometimes it can be helpful to understand what the reasons are behind these experiences. I wonder if we could spend some time trying to identify all of the possible explanations for the things that you are experiencing. You have told me that it could be due to a number of things, although you seemed unsure and appeared to fluctuate in what you felt may be causing them. Would it be possible to get them all down on paper?

CLIENT: Okay.

THERAPIST: Well, could you give me some of the reasons you have considered are responsible for what you are experiencing?

CLIENT: I suppose the main thing is that it is God punishing me for things in my past or in past lives, but I also think that I might have a brain tumour. I suppose the other thing that I think is that I am going mad because you don't see dead bodies on top of your wardrobe if you are normal, do you? I think they are the main things that come to mind at the moment.

THERAPIST: Okay. Well, let's put them down on our list, so the first thing is that it could be God doing this to you, the second is that it could be a brain tumour causing these things and the third is that you may be going mad. Is that right?

CLIENT: Yes.

THERAPIST: Okay, is there anything else that could be causing this? Maybe something someone else has said to you?

CLIENT: Well, the doctor and others said that I have drug-induced psychosis because of all the speed I did years ago.

THERAPIST: Should I put that down as another possibility?

CLIENT: I suppose so, but I am not so sure about that. What do you think?

THERAPIST: Well, we could put it on our list and look at the possibility of all of them.

CLIENT: Okay then, put it down.

THERAPIST: Can you think of any other things that might be the cause of these things, however remote the possibility is? Is there anything we have discussed that springs to mind that may lead to this kind of thing?

CLIENT: Well, I suppose it could be stress or just my life in general.

THERAPIST: So, should I put down the stress in Kate's life as a possibility?

CLIENT: I suppose so.

THERAPIST: If that is everything then what can be really helpful is if we now go through each of these possibilities and rate them from 0–100. Zero being that there is no possibility of this causing the things that are happening and 100 being that you are absolutely certain that this is the reason for these experiences.

A form to enable this process can be seen in Appendix 2 (see p. 126).

When ratings have been established for each of the explanations for the intrusions the next step should be to understand what emotions each of them lead to. At this stage, a formulation can be developed with each of the possibilities inserted and worked through to develop an understanding of what emotions and behaviours would follow from each alternative. Typically, this will produce a range of different emotions and behaviours. This can be a useful step in enabling the person to recognise the importance of interpretations of events, as opposed to events themselves, in determining emotional and behavioural reactions.

Subsequently, each of the explanations for the intrusions can be evaluated using a range of techniques, such as behavioural experiments or generating evidence for and against in order to establish the accuracy of the belief. After you have undertaken this process, beliefs about the explanations for the intrusion and emotions associated should be re-rated in order to establish any changes in conviction or intensity.

CASE EXAMPLE

A young woman, Kate (mentioned above), presented to the GP complaining of visual disturbances and beliefs that people were trying to harm her. Kate felt she may have a brain tumour and that this was causing her to lose control and she also worried about going mad. She was referred to a psychologist in primary care who saw her for two sessions and concurred that she should have a brain scan in order to rule out a tumour, but felt that her experiences were most likely to be induced by prolonged drug use. She was then referred to the Community Mental Health Team and she was seen by a CPN for an assessment session and, again, was given advice that there seemed to be little that their service could offer, but that she should, perhaps, continue to take her medication (antidepressants). She was subsequently referred to our team. At the initial meetings, Kate was extremely concerned that she did not want to be passed around any more and was very keen that she got some help, and that this help was not in the form of medication. She was extremely reluctant to attend the initial appointments, believing that we would assess her and pass her on without attempting any intervention.

At the initial assessment, it transpired that her main concerns were that she occasionally saw things at night such as a dead body on the top of her wardrobe, and felt that people were following her, and hearing noises. Interestingly, it appeared that Kate had a few possible explanations for her experiences, including going mad, a brain tumour and others. Her belief in the fact that it was a brain tumour was one that gave her some relief from her distress, because this meant that something could be done to assist with her problems and strange experiences, even if this was in the form of surgery. She recognised this as being slightly unusual, in that being happy to have a brain tumour is not what most people would report. However, what this clearly illustrates is the distress associated with her other beliefs regarding the nature of the experiences, particularly the belief that she was 'going mad'. Also of interest is that Kate only came up with stress and her life as a very last option, after a lengthy period of guided discussion (see abridged version above). She did not appear to consider this interpretation very often, despite actually believing this alternative very strongly. She was more preoccupied with the other explanations.

Kate had experienced a significant amount of stress in her life beginning at an early age. When she was three years of age she was left alone with her baby sister who was only three months old. Her mother had gone out to a local pub and her father was out at work. When her father returned from work to see that the Moses basket was lying on the floor upside down, he thought nothing of it, but heard crying upstairs and went to investigate. He found Kate under a pile of clothing extremely upset. They went downstairs and at that point he turned over the Moses basket to find the dead baby still in the basket. Kate was subsequently taken away from her parents whilst an investigation from social services took place. At the foster home she was frequently locked in a cupboard under the stairs, and on one of these occasions her biological parents arrived to see her. When they saw what was happening they immediately removed her from the foster parents.

Her mother has blamed Kate for the death of the baby over the years, saying that she must have knocked it off the side of the settee. This is clearly devastating for Kate and she finds it very hard to talk about.

When Kate was about 14 she was sexually abused, although she does not describe it in a traumatic sense. It appears that the man used to buy her things and make her feel special, and she describes that in some ways the sexual act itself was not that bad. However, she recently came into contact with this man again and he had assaulted another girl, this time being aggressive and violent. This led Kate to feel guilty that she had not done anything about it. There were other difficulties surrounding her relationship, and she lived in a run-down area. Considered together, these factors amounted to a significant amount of stress.

Once the range of alternatives was generated, each explanation was placed within the formulation. Using guided discovery, Kate was helped to recognise that the same experience can lead to a range of explanations, and that these are associated with different moods, which are dependent on the interpretation adopted. This mood can then be incorporated on the form for generating alternatives. The alternative explanations for Kate's experiences can be seen in Figure 8.1.

The formulation was developed for each of the beliefs and what this would entail in terms of emotions and behaviours. The first of these can be seen in Figure 8.2.

Another formulation is shown in Figure 8.3, with an alternative belief about the symptoms and subsequent behaviours and emotions.

Intrusive thought identified	I have been seeing things like dead bodies or images of myself hung in my wardrobe
Current explanation for thought and belief rating	I am going mad/have a brain tumour
Current mood associated with this belief	Frightened/happy

It can be helpful if we look at all of the possible explanations for this thought. I am aware that you have indicated the belief above as being the main reason for this although if there are any other alternatives for this I would be very keen to understand them.

Explanation for intrusion	*Belief rating (0–100)* 0 = this is not the reason I am having this thought 100 = this is definitely the reason I am having this thought	*Associated mood* Generated through formulation
God punishing me for something I have done in a previous life	40%	Frightened
Ghosts	75%	Scared
Brain tumour	100%	Doesn't bother me
Other people trying to harm me	5%	Scared
Going mad	85%	Depends, either okay or very frightened
Perhaps stress and Kate's life	90%	Unsure

Figure 8.1   Explanations for experiences form

Evidence for and against each of these explanations can then be examined. This can be accomplished using a combination of Socratic dialogue (a range of questions that can be used to evaluate beliefs is listed below) and/or behavioural experiments. Each of the explanations should be targeted in this way in an attempt to evaluate the explanation in a scientific manner. An example of evidence for and against Kate's explanations is given in Figure 8.4.

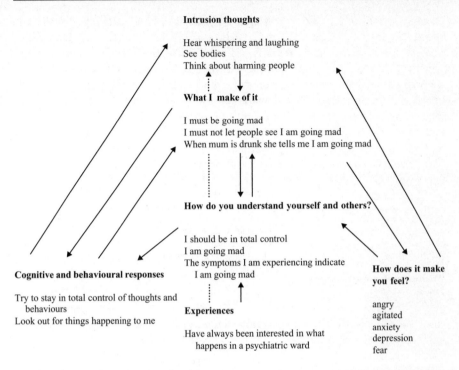

Figure 8.2 Idiosyncratic formulation indicating the importance of interpretation of intrusions in a catastrophic manner

Useful Questions to Help Evaluate Alternative Explanations

Counter evidence

- What counter evidence do I have that contradicts this explanation?
- Do I have any evidence that shows this explanation is not 100% true all of the time?

Someone else has the same explanation

- If my best friend, or someone close to me, explained things to me in this way, what would I say to them?

Another opinion

- What would someone else say to me about this explanation?
- If my best friend, or someone close to me, knew I was thinking this way, then what would they say to me?
- What evidence would they use to suggest that my explanation was not 100% true all of the time?

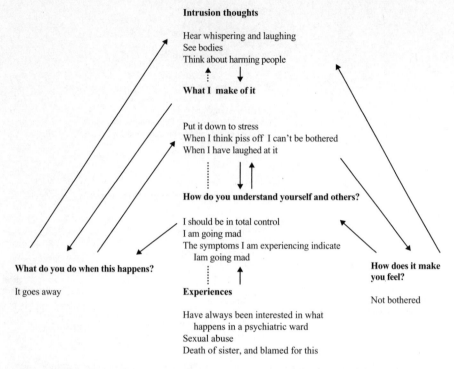

Figure 8.3 Idiosyncratic formulation indicating the importance of interpretation of intrusions using normalising information

Experiences

- What have I learnt from the past?
- Is there anything about the past that could have influenced how I am making sense of things at the moment?
- Have I ever believed something before with 100% conviction and it has turned out to be wrong?

Thinking errors

- Could I be making errors in my thinking?
- Am I jumping to conclusions that are not completely justified by the evidence?
- Am I forgetting, discounting or minimising relevant facts?
- Am I thinking in all-or-nothing terms?
- In reality, is it more likely that there are shades of grey?
- Am I being misled by how I feel inside, instead of focusing on the facts?

Belief to be examined *Associated mood* *Belief rating*	I have a brain tumour Doesn't bother me 100%

Evidence for	*Evidence against*
I am having lots of strange experiences.	People who have a brain tumour get progressively worse.
People with a brain tumour have strange experiences.	I have been getting better.
I have bad headaches at times.	I have been learning to make sense of these experiences.
	When I make sense of them they reduce and go away, this would not be the case if it was a brain tumour.
	My headaches usually respond to paracetamol, which I suppose would have very little effect on a brain tumour.

Belief rating (re-rated) *Alternative belief*	70% Maybe things are more related to stress which I suppose would also explain the headaches
Associated mood	More relaxed

Figure 8.4 Evidence for and against a belief

Safety behaviours

- Am I doing anything that could be maintaining this explanation?
- What am I doing to prevent this from happening? Does this stop me from finding out if it is true?
- Is there something I could do but feel too worried to do it, which would give me evidence to challenge this explanation?

Following this process, each of the explanations should be rated in terms of the level of conviction, in order to evaluate which explanation is most likely to be the most accurate based on all of the available evidence. This process of generating and evaluating alternative explanations for the symptoms experienced has proved an effective intervention for this client group.

SUMMARY

As discussed in the previous chapter, psychotic phenomena are a common experience within the general population, but it is the culturally unacceptable interpretation of these intrusions which leads to the person being labelled as psychotic. In this chapter, we have emphasised the importance of examining the interpretation of these intrusions and the subsequent cognitive, emotional and behavioural responses.

The process relies upon the therapist utilising Socratic dialogue in order to assist the client in developing a comprehensive list of possibilities for their intrusions with belief ratings and subsequent emotional consequences. These should then be incorporated within the formulation to assist in the process of recognising other behavioural or cognitive consequences associated with these appraisals. Examining evidence for and against distressing appraisals can be effective in reducing distress.

9

SAFETY BEHAVIOURS

There is evidence to suggest that people with anxiety disorders adopt certain behaviours in order to prevent some feared catastrophe (Clark, 1996; Salkovskis, 1991, 1996; Wells et al., 1995). The model of psychosis utilised throughout this book (Morrison, 2001) implicates cognitive and behavioural responses, including safety behaviours, in the maintenance of distress. Safety behaviours, whether cognitive or behavioural in nature, can serve to maintain dysfunctional interpretations of intrusions. Therefore, a full exploration of safety behaviours should be undertaken, and they should be considered in detail. If they appear to be involved in the maintenance of problematic interpretations, then experiments can be employed in order to help the client evaluate their short-term and long-term utility. In this chapter, we will consider some of the safety behaviours that we have observed with high-risk clients and some of the experiments that we have undertaken.

ASSESSMENT OF SAFETY BEHAVIOURS

A thorough assessment should be undertaken in order to explore all aspects of a person's safety behaviours. When working with panic patients, the best way to achieve this is to induce panic-like symptoms in order to observe what the person does to prevent the onset of a panic attack (Wells, 1997); similar strategies can be utilised with clients who are considered at risk of psychosis. It can be useful to see what the individual does in a situation where they consider themselves at risk of losing control or being in a feared situation that may induce symptoms. Encouraging an individual to lose control in an attempt to induce the onset of madness can also be useful, although people are frequently extremely uncomfortable about taking part in this type of experiment because of the feared outcome. Therefore, using other more accessible and less feared situations can have greater success in the initial stages of challenging safety behaviours. It can be useful to go with the individual into a feared situation, or induce a similar situation in session, so that safety behaviours can be observed. Some examples of events, their interpretation and subsequent safety behaviours can be seen in Figure 9.1.

Experience	Interpretation	Safety behaviour
Saw people laughing whilst out walking.	People in the street are talking about me.	To keep head down, walk fast and purposefully.
Visual hallucinatory experience, seeing a man sat on a chair.	I am going mad.	Not to look at the chair and get out of the room as quickly as possible.
Shopkeeper looking at me.	They know I am going mad.	Say very little (if I talk it will confirm I am going mad).
Visual hallucination of dead body on wardrobe.	I am going mad/losing control.	Hide head under covers.

Figure 9.1 Examples of safety behaviours

EXPERIMENTING WITH SAFETY BEHAVIOURS

Clearly, these behaviours lend themselves to experiments in order to test out whether they are useful. However, participation in experiments of this kind requires the individual to have some belief in the model, or at least in the fact that their behaviours may be maintaining some of these beliefs. There are numerous metaphors that cognitive therapists have developed and utilised over the years that can help to sell the concept of safety behaviours. These metaphors are shared with clients in order to help convey the concept of safety behaviours and how they may maintain a problematic belief. Some of the stories include the village of vampires, the man keeping elephants off train tracks by tearing up paper, or a workman holding up a wall to prevent it from falling down (see Wells, 1997, for further details). The first of these stories is described below:

There is a remote village in the depths of Transylvania and all of the villagers believe in vampires. They believe in vampires so much that all of the villagers keep strings of garlic around their necks at all times in order to keep the vampires away. They do this because, as everyone knows, vampires are afraid of garlic. The villagers have always done this for as long as anyone can remember, and no one in the village has ever seen or been attacked by a vampire. Because no one has seen a vampire, they know that the garlic is working. They would never want to be without their garlic as this may allow the vampires into the village.

Once the story has been told a number of questions could be asked:

- What do you make of the villagers' belief about the vampires?
- What do you make of the villagers' belief about the garlic?
- Are there any problems with their situation? How would they react if there were a shortage of garlic?
- How could the villagers find out whether vampires actually exist?
- Are there any similarities between some of the things you do and the garlic used by the villagers?
- What could you do in order to test out these behaviours?
- How would you go about that?

These questions utilise a Socratic approach to enable the individual to recognise that their behaviours may have a similar effect to that of the garlic for the villagers (i.e. it makes them feel safe in the short term, but may keep them believing in a distressing idea in the long term). Such stories can, at times, enable the person to have sufficient courage to try out an experiment. This may, initially, be a very small test or change of behaviours, and may require the individual to engage in testing their behaviours within session before they can get the confidence to attempt this outside of the therapy sessions.

In order to examine assessment and treatment in greater depth, a specific case will be discussed in order to examine how safety behaviours may become established and, as in anxiety disorders, maintain the problem.

CASE EXAMPLE (1)

Henry, a 26-year-old man, was referred to the project after being assessed by a local casualty department, which he reluctantly attended at the persuasion of his relatives, who felt that he had become increasingly anxious, angry and unpredictable. In casualty, the staff felt uncertain about his presentation, although they felt that he might meet the criteria for our project. In view of this, he was referred to the study and also for an outpatient appointment with a consultant psychiatrist. The initial assessment took place a few days after the referral when he was seen at the family home where he lived. Henry was quite reluctant to discuss his problems, although his family (who were very keen to be involved) prompted Henry to disclose some of the difficulties he had been experiencing. After the initial assessment, Henry felt that there was no need to be involved with the project. Despite this, his family maintained telephone contact with the project team and were concerned that he should receive some kind of help and they wanted to learn ways of managing some of the difficulties he was experiencing.

By maintaining contact with the family, Henry eventually agreed (although still quite reluctantly) to meet with the therapist in the project. The initial meetings were spent engaging Henry in therapy. Many of the techniques discussed in Chapter 5 such as negotiating the time and location of meetings, using a shared language, and demonstrating a willingness to listen and understand were utilised alongside a guided-discovery questioning style, which enabled Henry to think about the development of his difficulties. Henry began to acknowledge that something had been wrong and that he had been under a lot of stress although he wanted to forget about his problems. This was consistent with a sealing-over coping style as described by McGlashan (1987).

Despite wanting to forget about his psychological problems, a shared problem list allowed Henry to prioritise the things that he could work on:

1. Wanting more money
2. Wanting a job
3. What happened

The therapist suggested problem number 3, and it was agreed that this could be put on the problem list, although at that time it was viewed as a low priority. Henry also saw the psychiatrist around this time and, following the appointment, Henry and his father felt there had been little opportunity to discuss matters and he was subsequently discharged from psychiatric care. Significantly, Henry had been adamant that he did not wish to take medication as a treatment option, but was content with a psychological intervention strategy and appeared to be gradually engaging with the therapist as time went on and trust was established.

It transpired that at the point that he was having his 'breakdown', Henry had been reasonably convinced that people were following him. Henry reported that he had developed this belief after seeing a camera move, which had appeared to follow his movements late one night in a car park. Subsequently, he began to believe that people he knew may be controlling these cameras. This belief was then maintained, because friends and relatives really did start to keep an eye on Henry (because of their concerns about his increasingly erratic behaviour). Henry picked up on the concerns of family and friends, but also became convinced that other people were following him (because of selective attention to and monitoring of the speech and behaviour of other people). Henry agreed to spend some time examining evidence in relation to specific situations, in an attempt to discriminate between factual evidence and unsubstantiated conclusions. A critical incident was identified, which had occurred when he had driven to a friend's house some distance away. During this journey, he became concerned that a large number of people who were also driving on the motorway had been monitoring his progress throughout the journey. Henry believed that these people had been instructed to do so by a specific person. It transpired that his evidence supporting this belief was that people had looked at him whilst he was driving on the motorway. In an effort to examine whether this appeared to be the correct interpretation of these experiences, Henry was asked questions surrounding his belief. Questions about the belief – such as the number of people required for this conspiracy to succeed, the difficulty of organising them, and the costs involved – were carefully explored. When working with psychotic clients, this is termed *peripheral questioning* (Kingdon & Turkington, 1994). Previously, Henry had not considered these peripheral aspects of his belief, and he quickly began to consider alternative explanations for the experiences he described. Over time, other incidents that had previously led Henry to believe that there was some form of conspiracy involving him were examined in a similar way. The process of challenging these beliefs was emphasised so that Henry could utilise this strategy himself (analogous to becoming his own therapist).

Later sessions were spent working on Henry's problem of wanting a job. Although he did secure a job, it paid significantly less than his previous one prior to his illness. The process of rehabilitation was discussed in the context of a physical illness and how this may be pertinent to his situation; however, despite this it became apparent that experiences of loss and rejection had led to depressive thoughts. Henry also disclosed that he experienced suicidal thoughts, although these had been highly intrusive in nature. He was clear that he had no desire to end his life, but worried that, if he had these thoughts for long enough, he was bound to act on them. Normalising information about intrusive thoughts was important (as discussed in Chapter 7), and this was provided, based on the paper by Rachman and De Silva (1978). This process challenged the catastrophic interpretations of his suicidal thoughts, which led to a reduction in the frequency, duration, distress and preoccupation associated with these thoughts.

Henry was close to being discharged from therapy when a close friend died suddenly. Whilst Henry was drinking in a local pub with friends who knew the deceased, he started to experience symptoms similar to those experienced during a panic attack. Following this and combined with his previous experiences and the family history he started to believe that he was 'going mad'. To prevent others from seeing that he was 'going mad' he started to avoid people and increasingly isolated himself. At this point his sleep pattern deteriorated as he spent long periods of time awake at night worrying about what was happening to him. In the session immediately following this event, Henry was clearly having difficulty communicating and his speech was slow and vague.

It took some time to isolate what his concerns were but eventually thoughts associated with the panic attack, and the key catastrophic misinterpretation of 'I am going mad', were discussed. It was also clear that his behaviours of reduced speech and social isolation were safety behaviours, designed to prevent the outward signs of madness from being recognised by others (this is similar to the conceptualisation of negative symptoms as safety behaviours; see Morrison et al., 2003). A formulation of these behaviours and experiences was presented to Henry. Audiotapes were utilised to record sessions on a regular basis, and this enabled an experiment to be set up to test out one of his safety behaviours regarding his slow, considered speech, which he believed prevented others from seeing he was going mad. In the session a typical experiment was set up, in which Henry was encouraged to manipulate his safety behaviours and then observe how he communicated by reviewing the tape. During the experiment Henry was asked to try out three conditions:

1. His current method of communication, which utilised slow, considered speech. He was asked to maintain this for five minutes.
2. He was to increase his safety behaviours and exaggerate them (if they are helpful doing more of them may make things even better), and maintain this condition for a further five minutes.
3. Lastly, he was to drop all safety behaviours and communicate as he would have done previously; again, for five minutes.

At the end of this process the tape was reviewed, and both he and the therapist discussed how his communication skills had appeared in each of the conditions. It was blatantly obvious, after reviewing the tape, that his speech whilst maintaining his safety behaviours appeared disjointed, uncertain and awkward. This became further exaggerated in the next condition, where he increased his safety behaviours. In the final condition, when his safety behaviours were dropped, his speech appeared much more relaxed and comfortable. After this experiment, Henry felt that his original belief about his slow, considered speech might, in fact, have produced the opposite effect. His behaviours could have been considered as negative symptoms and would have given people cause for concern; however, their initial function was to prevent people becoming concerned about him. Subsequently, we discussed other behaviours, such as isolation, and Henry agreed that these might have a similar effect. He decided that they might not be as useful as he had originally thought.

Henry quickly recovered from this episode, significantly reducing his safety behaviours and increasing his activity levels. His worries declined about 'going mad', which, alongside his increased activities, assisted with his sleep problem.

At the end of his contact with the project, Henry had obtained a job similar to the one he had prior to the emergence of his symptoms. He had no further suicidal thoughts and he recognised the process of therapy and how this should be implemented. Henry was provided with an 'early warning signs' package and a blueprint of therapy. This was provided on audiotape, since this is the media Henry preferred (as opposed to written material).

SELECTIVE ATTENTION AS A SAFETY BEHAVIOUR

Selective attention has frequently been identified as a safety behaviour, in our experience of working with this client group, and is usually implicated in the maintenance of distressing interpretations, as would be predicted by the S-REF model of emotional dysfunction (Wells & Matthews, 1994). If we consider the above case, Henry was clearly concerned about the impending onset of madness and wanted to avoid letting others see he was going mad. He therefore initiated his safety behaviours and looked for signs of others perceiving him as 'going mad'. He reported frequently seeing other people looking at him and that they were looking at him oddly.

In this example, his safety behaviours, in conjunction with selective attention, contributed to the maintenance of the problems. His safety behaviours increased the chances of people actually looking at him. Selective attention only allows him to register those people who do look at him, and ensures that he fails to process the people who do not look at him for various reasons. One of the aims of treatment would be to highlight the vicious circles that are operating and maintaining this problem.

In treatment, we frequently draw on existing techniques (Wells, 1997) that highlight selective attention and how it may well contribute to the maintenance of problems. There are a number of ways of enabling a person to recognise the effects of selective attention. One way is to discuss the idea of selective attention in therapy by highlighting the way that it works. Simply asking the individual to concentrate on their bottom, and how it feels on their chair, can begin to illustrate the processes involved. When you ask someone to do this, they immediately start to notice sensations in their bottom that they were previously unaware of. This illustrates that, once attention is directed towards something, you will notice much more information about it. Asking if these sensations have only just begun can start to illustrate the fact that we have mental filters, which operate to disregard information that is not considered pertinent at the time. This does not mean that the information is not available; rather, that we choose not to pay attention to it. Some education about filter mechanisms of attention can also be useful.

Another method of demonstrating the effects of selective attention is to find something significant that has changed in the person's life, such as becoming pregnant, or the purchase of a new car. The usual line of questioning would be something like:

- Before X happened, how many did you notice?
- After X happened, how many did you notice?
- Do you think that there were actually more of X?
- What do you think was the reason for this?
- Could it be that your attention was directed to look out for X?
- What do you make of this?
- Could anything similar be happening with your current concerns?

This line of questioning allows the individual to recognise that what is happening to them is part of a normal process. Their attention may be directed by their current concerns, and this may increase the frequency of an occurrence being noticed, rather than the actual frequency of this occurrence.

Behavioural experiments can be undertaken to test out the effects of selective attention. Simple experiments, such as asking the person to tell you how many post boxes they pass on the way to the appointment or how many people wear certain kinds of trainers, can assist in enabling clients to understand attentional processes. In these examples, they should be encouraged to provide an estimate of the number of post boxes or how many people may wear certain types of trainers. The experimental part encourages them to specifically look out for these things and record the actual number. This should be discussed in the following week's homework review. Frequently, people are surprised at the number of times they have noticed a specific thing once their attention has been directed towards it. This can then be discussed in relation to their own experiences.

CASE EXAMPLE (2)

A young man, Peter, was referred to the project with beliefs centring on the film *The Truman Show*. In this film, Truman Burbank has a nice house with a white picket fence, set in the idyllic oceanside community of Seahaven; a loyal wife; an even more loyal best friend; and a cushy desk job. Unbeknown to Truman, the entire life he has lived is mere programming for a 24-hour television network. Seahaven is one large soundstage, where all events are scripted and all the inhabitants are actors (i.e. except for Truman, who was adopted as an infant by the Omnicam Corporation, and has had every step of his life traced and moulded by the show's creator). Since seeing this film, Peter started to wonder if a similar experience could be happening to him, although this was a fleeting thought.

However, other things seemed to be happening around the same time, such as the UK Channel 4 television programme *Big Brother*, in which 10 people live together in a house and are filmed 24 hours a day for television. This served to exacerbate his concerns about being watched, and he increasingly searched for any evidence to support his beliefs. Around this time he was walking down the road when someone called his name very clearly ('Hey, Peter!') as he was walking towards them. The person who called his name did not approach him, but walked straight past him, despite giving him a sideways glance. Peter appraised this as evidence that other people knew who he was and that he may be famous. As a consequence, his beliefs in *The Truman Show* increased. He felt that he should try to collect more evidence to support his theory that people knew him, which would in turn support his *Truman Show* hypothesis. He started to look around at people out of the corner of his eye, and if he caught glimpses of people looking at him, then this reinforced his beliefs and

GENERATING ALTERNATIVES

Name: *Peter*   **Date:** *26. 12. 01*

Intrusive thought   *People look at me when I am out on the street*
identified

Current explanation   *I am in a kind of 'Truman Show';*
for thought; belief   *belief rating 80%*
rating

Current mood associated   *Anxious*
with this belief

It can be helpful if we look at all of the possible explanations for this thought. I
am aware that you have indicated the belief above as being the main reason for
this although if there are any other alternatives for this I would be very keen to
understand them.

Explanation for intrusion	Belief rating (1–100) 1 = this is not the reason I am having this thought 100 = this is definitely the reason I am having this thought	Associated mood
The Truman Show	80%	Anxious/fear
Previous drug use	60–75%	Scared
Stressed and confused	40%	More relaxed

Figure 9.2   Form for generating alternatives

he would quickly avert his eyes. As he began to accumulate this evidence, he became
more and more anxious and confused; this was the point at which he was referred to
the team.

The initial sessions focused on assessment and developing a list of problems and
goals. Peter believed that his experiences could be potentially due to a number of
things and these were explored using the generating alternatives form and can be seen
in Figure 9.2. Also, at this point he was introduced to the concept of safety behaviours
and selective attention.

After being exposed to the inductive methods associated with CT, and the concepts
of selective attention and safety behaviours, Peter decided to undertake a different
experiment to test out his beliefs that people were watching him.

He had started to feel more uncertain as to whether people were watching him or whether this could be his mistaken perception of things because of misinterpreting normal social cues. He felt that he should test this out, and decided that he should try to see what it would be like if he was entirely sure that people were looking at him. He could then compare this with his current experiences, and see if there were any differences. He wondered what he could do to ensure that people looked at him and to eliminate any uncertainty. Eventually, he decided to dye his hair green and then go out, which he felt should attract sufficient attention from others. He planned to go out in the morning with his normal hair colour, and then go out again in the afternoon with green hair. When he did this, he noticed a significant difference in not only the number of people looking at him, but also the quality of the experience. Previously, he had felt that glances were an indication of people looking at him; however, following the experiment he was able to distinguish the difference between normal social interactions and people actively looking at him. This experiment served to indicate that he was potentially misinterpreting data and enhanced his awareness of the need to subject such experiences to greater scrutiny.

ACTIVITY SCHEDULING TO COMBAT AVOIDANCE

Avoidance is commonly used as a safety behaviour in order to prevent a feared outcome (such as 'going mad', worsening of symptoms or humiliation). Frequently, in the development of psychosis, people can become preoccupied with their experiences or fearful of what others may say (Moller & Husby, 2000). This can lead to an enforced isolation, where people spend increasing amounts of time alone, perhaps in their room. This reduction in frequency and duration of contact they have with other people can lead to increased preoccupation with their experiences and thoughts. Such isolation can also reduce the possibility for external sources of generating and evaluating alternatives, which has been suggested to contribute to the development of psychosis (French et al., 2001). The isolation can also lead to increased feelings of depression. The use of activity scheduling can be a valuable means of monitoring and impacting upon activity levels. Frequently, individuals feel that the isolation is a consequence of their difficulties; however, it can also be a maintaining factor. Encouraging people to become more active can be a significant step forward. However, this is usually best achieved through behavioural experiments rather than direct instruction. Initially, the individual should be encouraged to chart their levels of activity on an activity schedule (see Appendix 4 for a suitable template, p. 129). During the activity, individuals should be encouraged to rate themselves on two dimensions:

- the level of mastery associated with the task in hand
- the amount of pleasure associated with the task (Beck et al., 1979).

Undertaking this baseline assessment frequently demonstrates that periods of inactivity can often be related to reduced levels of mood. It can also be the case that reduced levels of activity can also be associated with increased levels of psychotic experience. Setting up an experiment to test the effects of increased activity levels on someone's mood and frequency of psychotic experiences can be an effective means of increasing activity levels, with an accompanying reduction in psychotic experiences and increase in mood.

SUMMARY

Throughout this chapter we have emphasised the importance of safety behaviours as described in the anxiety literature and their similar contribution in the model of psychosis presented. These safety behaviours, whether cognitive or behavioural in nature, can serve to maintain dysfunctional interpretations of intrusions. Thorough assessment is required, which may necessitate the induction of a feared situation in session in order to explore all aspects of a person's safety behaviours. The importance of testing these behaviours through experiments is discussed and case material is utilised to emphasise the approach.

This chapter also examines the role of selective attention as a specific behaviour frequently utilised by this client group and again utilises case material to highlight the role of this behaviour in the maintenance of distress.

Finally, we discuss avoidance and encourage activity scheduling as a useful intervention to combat this behaviour.

10

METACOGNITIVE BELIEFS

In the cognitive conceptualisation of anxiety disorders there is increasing recognition that metacognition is an important factor. Wells and Matthews (1994) have proposed a self-regulatory executive function (S-REF) model of emotional disorders, and several specific cognitive models of anxiety disorder have been developed incorporating elements of this (e.g. generalised anxiety disorder; Wells, 1995). The S-REF model suggests that vulnerability to psychological dysfunction is associated with a cognitive-attentional syndrome characterised by heightened self-focused attention, attentional bias, ruminative processing and activation of dysfunctional beliefs. In this model, cognitive-attentional experiences such as biased information processing and cognitive intrusions are mediated by executive processes that are directed by the patient's beliefs. Some beliefs are metacognitive in nature and, as such, are linked to the interpretation, selection and execution of particular thought processes and strategies. Wells (1995) states that metacognitive beliefs include beliefs about thought processes (e.g. 'I have a poor memory'); the advantages and disadvantages of certain types of thinking (e.g. 'My worrying could make me go mad'); and beliefs about the content of thoughts (e.g. 'It is bad to think about death'). Discussing such beliefs in reference to generalised anxiety disorder and obsessive-compulsive disorder, Wells (1995) argues that in these patients, it is their appraisal of and response to their cognitive processes that distinguishes them from non-clinical samples, as opposed to the content of their cognitions.

The model of psychosis described throughout this manual directs treatment towards working with metacognition (Morrison, 2001). Positive beliefs may generate additional intrusions, whilst negative appraisals of unusual experiences as being dangerous or uncontrollable may initiate or accelerate the progression to psychosis. In the next section positive and negative beliefs will be discussed in more detail.

POSITIVE BELIEFS

There is considerable empirical support for the involvement of positive beliefs about unusual experiences in the development of psychosis. Miller, O'Connor and

DiPasquale (1993) found that 50% of inpatients reported some positive effects relating to their hallucinations, with the most commonly cited benefits including hallucinations being relaxing or soothing or providing companionship. In another study of voice hearers, Chadwick and Birchwood (1994) also found that if people appraised their voices as being benevolent then these voices were engaged. In non-patients, Morrison, Wells and Nothard (2000) found that positive beliefs about unusual experiences were the best predictor of predisposition to auditory and visual hallucinations. Therefore, it is clear that positive beliefs may be implicated in progression to psychosis for those who experience hallucinatory phenomena. It is also common to find patients who hold positive beliefs regarding their delusions, particularly in the early stages (obviously important for our client group). For example, persecutory ideas may add meaning to the person's life, making them special, may provide excitement (something often lacking from a psychiatric patient's existence) or may defend against self-blame, as suggested by Bentall, Kinderman and Kaney (1994). Paranoia can also be viewed as a useful survival strategy.

There are many clinical examples from our patients that illustrate the importance of such positive beliefs, and the subsequent adoption of strategies, in the development of psychosis. For example, people may take substances, such as cannabis, ecstasy or cocaine, in order to deliberately induce paranoia or hallucinatory phenomena. Several patients have begun to deliberately allocate attention to such phenomena, in order to increase their frequency. It is also evident that, for some people, such phenomena may occur as a coping response in relation to trauma or traumatic memories, as noted by Romme and Escher (1989).

Strategies that can be used to help reduce distress that is associated with metacognitive beliefs are the same as could be used with other beliefs. For example, strategies such as evaluating evidence, generating alternative explanations, behavioural experiments and considering the advantages and disadvantages of holding a particular belief can all be used to work with metacognitive beliefs. A typical positive belief about unusual experiences or beliefs would be that, 'paranoia is useful and helps you stay out of danger'. For such a belief, any of the above may be useful. A sensible place to start would be to evaluate the accuracy of such a statement by considering the advantages and disadvantages in two columns.

Examples

Carl, a 19-year-old male with a level of suspiciousness and paranoia that met our criteria for attenuated symptoms, endorsed the belief that his paranoia was functional. He cited that his paranoia and hypervigilance kept him out of danger, and reported several occasions when he believed he would have been assaulted if he had not been alert. Given that the area in which he lived was highly deprived and had significant levels of street crime and violence, this perception may well have been accurate. He had also been involved in the selling of illicit drugs, and felt that paranoia was an occupational requirement. However, he also recognised that there were times when he was unable to leave the house without discomfort because of his suspiciousness, which was problematic. We collaboratively generated an alternative 'rulebook' regarding when it was necessary to be suspicious and when he could relax, which maintained his perceived benefits but reduced the associated costs.

Another common positive belief is the valuing of hallucinatory phenomena. For example, Kylie, a 22-year-old female with infrequent verbal auditory hallucinations, actually enjoyed hearing the voices. They had mixed content (some positive and some negative), and invariably occurred at night when she was in bed. She believed, at the time of hearing them, that they were either ghosts (of the friendly variety) or other people using telepathy. In sessions, she believed that they were hallucinations or tricks of her mind. She derived several advantages from the voices, including advice (she would ask questions sub-vocally and they would respond with single-word answers) and companionship. Thus, she was encouraged to explore alternative sources of these benefits, such as discussing some issues with her sister and trying to meet new people by joining an evening class.

NEGATIVE BELIEFS

Positive beliefs about unusual experiences would appear to be linked to the occurrence of such experiences. It is only when these experiences are appraised as uncontrollable or dangerous, or lead to negative environmental consequences (such as problems with occupational and social functioning), that they become problematic (Morrison et al., 2002) and contribute to the development of a psychotic disorder that involves distress and disability.

Baker and Morrison (1998) found that patients experiencing auditory hallucinations scored higher on metacognitive beliefs concerning beliefs about uncontrollability and danger associated with certain types of thoughts. In addition, Freeman and Garety (1999) found that the majority of a sample of people with persecutory delusions experienced meta-worry concerning the control of delusional ideas. Similarly, Chadwick and Birchwood (1994) reported that patients who believe their voices to be benevolent try to resist them.

If patients are progressing towards a psychotic disorder, it is highly likely that they are beginning to make negative interpretations of unusual experiences or beliefs. These may be to do with loss of control or going mad (as suggested by Morrison, 1998b), or viewing the experiences as coming from someone or something powerful and malevolent (as suggested by Chadwick and Birchwood, 1994). If this is the case, then standard CT strategies can be used to evaluate the accuracy of these negative interpretations.

In people at high risk of developing psychosis, it is clear that negative beliefs about unusual experiences or thoughts may be implicated in the progression to psychosis. In our study, it was evident that the high-risk patients scored significantly higher than non-patients on all of the negative belief subscales of the MCQ (Morrison et al., 2002), including beliefs about uncontrollability of thoughts, beliefs about superstition, punishment and responsibility and self-conscious beliefs.

A common negative belief is that thinking, imagining or dreaming about something bad can make it happen (cf. thought–action fusion; Rachman, 1997). For example, Joe, a 19-year-old man, believed that the dreams that he had were likely to come true. This was problematic, since they frequently involved harm to his friends and family (such as car crashes, physical assaults or terminal illnesses). He believed this because he had, on several occasions, noticed dreaming about something that had happened the next day. Clearly, he had difficulty controlling his dreams, which caused him a great deal of distress. When presenting for therapy, he was actively trying to avoid sleeping, and had increased his use of caffeine, nicotine and amphetamines in order to achieve this. Behavioural experiments with dreams were difficult to generate, so he was encouraged to keep a diary of his dreams. It became apparent that, while some minor things that he had dreamed about occurred, there was no link between what he dreamt about and any real catastrophes. He was also encouraged to consider the mechanism by which such a process could occur, and he decided that if it worked with dreams it should really work with thoughts and images. He then decided to try to ensure that no goals were scored by any of the 92 Football League teams on a particular weekend; obviously, this did not happen, and he became much less preoccupied and distressed by his original concerns.

ASSESSMENTS OF METACOGNITION

In addition to clinical interviews for the assessment of metacognitive factors (see Wells, 2000), there are self-report measures that can be useful.

Meta-Cognitions Questionnaire

The *Meta-Cognitions Questionnaire* (MCQ; Cartwright-Hatton & Wells, 1997) is a useful measure both in terms of prediction of at-risk groups but also in terms of its clinical application. This is a 65-item measure of beliefs about mental events that has been shown to discriminate between patients experiencing auditory hallucinations, psychiatric controls and normal subjects (Baker & Morrison, 1998) and correlates with predisposition to psychotic symptoms in non-patients (Morrison, Wells & Nothard, 2000). It has been shown to differentiate people at high risk of psychosis from non-patients (Morrison et al., 2002). The questionnaire generates scores for the following five subscales:

1. Positive beliefs about worry (typical items include 'Worrying helps me to get things sorted out in my mind' and 'Worrying helps me cope')
2. Negative beliefs about the controllability of thoughts and corresponding danger (typical items include 'Worrying is dangerous for me' and 'I cannot ignore my worrying thoughts')
3. Cognitive confidence (typical items include 'I have a poor memory' and 'I have difficulty knowing if I have actually done something, or just imagined it')
4. Negative beliefs about thoughts in general, including responsibility, punishment and superstition (typical items include 'Not being able to control my thoughts is a sign of weakness' and 'If I did not control a worrying thought, and then it happened, it would be my fault')
5. Cognitive self-consciousness (typical items include 'I think a lot about my thoughts' and 'I pay close attention to the way my mind works').

Items are scored from 1 to 4, whereby 1 = *do not agree*, 2 = *agree slightly*, 3 = *agree moderately*, and 4 = *agree very much*.

Subscales exhibit good internal consistency (alphas ranged between 0.72 and 0.89) and test–retest reliability (coefficients ranged between 0.76 and 0.94).

Interpretations of Voices Inventory

Another self-report measure that may be useful in assessing positive and negative beliefs about hallucinatory experiences is the *Interpretations of Voices Inventory* (Morrison et al., 2002). This measure has been shown to identify positive and negative appraisals of auditory hallucinations in the general population. Positive interpretations of voices are associated with the frequency of hallucinatory phenomena, whereas negative interpretations are associated with distress (Morrison et al., 2002). It is a 26-item questionnaire that measures the beliefs that people hold about hearing voices. There are three subscales measuring metaphysical beliefs, positive beliefs and beliefs about loss of control. The questions are worded hypothetically ('If I were to hear sounds or voices that other people could not hear, I would probably think that . . .') and participants respond to each item by circling how much they agree with the statements about voices (1 = *not at all*, 2 = *somewhat*, 3 = *moderately so*, 4 = *very much*).

TREATMENT IMPLICATIONS

As suggested, the treatment of these beliefs should focus on reduction of distress. Strategies such as evaluating evidence, generating alternative explanations, behavioural experiments and considering advantages and disadvantages can all be utilised with metacognitive beliefs. It has also been discussed that a common experience is for people to believe that unusual cognitions indicate the onset of madness.

Reducing the frequency of these experiences is commonly a goal of individuals; for example, 'I do not want to think I am being followed' or 'I do not want to see things on top of my wardrobe at night'. This is often because of their metacognitive appraisal of such experiences; for example, 'If I think these things then I must be going mad'. To stop people from having the experience of misinterpreting things at night, when they are alone in a dark room and they are expecting something awful to happen, is beyond the scope of therapy. This is a normal reaction. However, helping people to evaluate whether these experiences indicate the onset of madness is something that is not beyond the scope of therapy. Often, helping people to evaluate their beliefs about such experiences can have an effect on reducing their occurrence. (For a description of the effects of changing appraisals and reducing suppression on the frequency of intrusions, see Wegner, 1994.) Therefore, targeting the metacognitive beliefs is essential in reducing the frequency of, and distress associated with, these beliefs. This process is extremely important for symptom and distress reduction, as well as for relapse prevention. It is feasible that the individual could be left with a reduction in distress and symptoms by altering behaviours or environmental aspects alone. However, the individual may still hold the belief that these experiences are in some way catastrophic. As discussed, many of these phenomena are part of normal human experience, so they are likely to recur at some point. This will trigger their metacognitive beliefs surrounding the catastrophic nature of these experiences and once again things could spiral out of control (see Gumley, White & Power, 1999). Therefore, it is important to assess and treat these beliefs.

SUMMARY

In this chapter metacognitive beliefs are discussed in terms of their importance regarding the maintenance and possible increase in frequency of, and distress associated with, intrusions. The way in which people consider their thoughts has been recognised as being important in the literature on anxiety disorders for some time, particularly OCD. Wells and Matthews (1994) argue that it is the appraisal of and response to such cognitive processes that distinguishes help-seeking patients from non-clinical samples, as opposed to the content of their cognitions. In psychosis, the appraisal of voices as being benevolent or malevolent has a clear link with distress (Chadwick & Birchwood, 1994). As discussed in Chapter 7, there is evidence that psychotic phenomena can be detected in the general population. What appears to distinguish the general population from the clinical population is the appraisal of these experiences (e.g. Peters, Joseph & Garety, 1999). The model presented throughout this book highlights the importance of both positive and negative beliefs about psychotic experiences. The chapter also highlights the importance of targeting these beliefs in order to effect long-term change since, if catastrophic metacognitive beliefs remain, this can leave the individual vulnerable to further episodes.

11

'I AM DIFFERENT' AND OTHER CORE BELIEFS

Our early experiences shape our core beliefs and, in many of our clients, it is not difficult to understand why their early experiences have led to them to develop core beliefs in which they view themselves as being somehow different to others. The model presented throughout this book incorporates faulty self and social knowledge; it is here that core beliefs are incorporated into formulations. The identification of core beliefs is vital in order to develop a comprehensive formulation. However, their modification may not always be necessary or indicated. The development of a formulation with the client, demonstrating how their beliefs have arisen, can in many cases be sufficient. However, for some individuals, core beliefs may be influential in maintaining their dysfunctional interpretations, or may represent significant vulnerability factors for future relapse, and modification may be necessary. If it appears necessary, it is important to obtain informed consent from the client, and to help them examine the advantages, as well as the disadvantages, associated with holding such beliefs.

A very common core belief, which has been highlighted in our work, is that people at risk of psychosis believe that they are different. This can be related to many early experiences, although common themes include bullying, rape/sexual abuse, threat towards the individual, or incidents that leave the individual feeling alone and vulnerable. They have often made sense of such experiences by assuming that it has occurred because they are different, or that they have become different as a result of what has happened. As described in the previous chapter, it is possible for people to interpret being different in a positive or a negative way.

IDENTIFICATION OF CORE BELIEFS

Core beliefs can be identified through a number of techniques, which have been developed for this purpose. The *downward arrow technique* is one of the most common ways of accessing these beliefs. This technique requires the therapist to take a negative thought from therapy and then spend time understanding why the individual may be experiencing that thought in relation to their core beliefs. The technique should be appropriately introduced. An example of this technique is demonstrated below.

CLIENT: When I am in the company of other people, I think it is better to keep quiet so there is less chance of people talking to me.

THERAPIST: You have mentioned things similar to this on other occasions. Would it be possible if I asked some questions about this thought to see if there is an underlying belief, which may be supporting these thoughts.

CLIENT: I suppose that would be okay, if you feel it would be useful.

THERAPIST: Well, should we try and see if it is helpful?

CLIENT: Okay.

THERAPIST: In relation to your original thought, you said that it was 'better to keep quiet so that people don't talk to you'. Could you tell me what would be the worst thing about someone talking to you?

CLIENT: Well, the attention would be on me and, as we have discussed, that is something I find really horrible.

THERAPIST: And could you tell me what would be the worst thing about people paying increased attention to you?

CLIENT: They would see me for who I am.

THERAPIST: And what would be the worst thing about that?

CLIENT: Well, they would see how weird and different I really am.

THERAPIST: So can I check that I understand – if people talked to you they may find out that you are in some way weird or different, is that right?

CLIENT: Well, yes.

THERAPIST: And what would be so bad about that?

CLIENT: If I'm weird and different, then other people won't be able to love me.

THERAPIST: So you worry that you are unlovable, because of being different?

CLIENT: Yes.

This process can quite readily give access to core beliefs. Some therapists feel that uncovering core beliefs can be a long and tortuous process. Whilst it should not be undertaken lightly, the process of identifying these beliefs can be straightforward in many cases. This process can generate several core beliefs (in the above example, 'I am weird and different' and 'I am unlovable'), and these can be examined in turn. A modified Dysfunctional Thought Record can be utilised to access core beliefs and role-play can also be useful.

MODIFICATION OF CORE BELIEFS

There are many existing techniques that have been developed for evaluating the accuracy of core beliefs. Consideration of evidence for and against a core belief is a common method of evaluating such beliefs, as are the generation of alternative explanations, role-play and flashcards. Padesky (1994) has also suggested techniques such as historical tests, positive data logs and the use of continua.

For many people, their beliefs about being weird or different and subsequent compensatory beliefs (as discussed in Chapter 6) reflect their early experiences. Their beliefs about being weird make sense, and their strategies to avoid being seen as weird appear functional when considered historically. However, operationalising weirdness and the associated compensatory strategies at the present time provides current material to help with evaluation. This is commonly undertaken in people with anxiety disorders, such as social phobia. For example, if people feel that they are going red, then it is important to find out how red they go, and shades of red from a colour pallet can be used for this purpose. The same is true for beliefs regarding weirdness, although they can be a little more difficult to define since there is not an easily defined pallet of weirdness to access. The following example illustrates this process:

THERAPIST:	I am aware that you think you are weird. What can be helpful, as we have previously done, is to see if we can find a way of measuring this in order to see if any changes take place. Is that okay?
CLIENT:	Yes, that's okay.
THERAPIST:	Well, how weird do you consider yourself to be? Let's use a scale of 0–100, with 0 being absolutely normal and no signs of weirdness and 100 is the weirdest you could possibly be.
CLIENT:	Well, I am obviously pretty strange, but I am not sure where I would rate myself. Perhaps about 80%.
THERAPIST:	Okay, well can you think of other people who we could place on a continuum between 0–100. Let's draw a line and place people on it according to weirdness. Do you know anyone who is totally ordinary and normal?
CLIENT:	Well, I suppose people like librarians spring to mind. They seem boring and normal; I can't imagine them to be particularly weird.
THERAPIST:	That's really useful. Where should we put librarians on this continuum from 0–100?
CLIENT:	Well, I suppose that they may be a bit strange but nothing major, about 10.
THERAPIST:	Okay, well what about particular individuals? Is there anyone you know personally, neighbours, friends, family, or even in the media who you would consider normal?
CLIENT:	I'm not sure, no one springs to mind.
THERAPIST:	What about someone who others see as being normal?
CLIENT:	I suppose Trevor McDonald is pretty normal, he was voted the person most people trust; I suppose you wouldn't trust a weirdo.
THERAPIST:	So where should we put Trevor McDonald on our line?
CLIENT:	Well, he would go around 5.

THERAPIST: Okay, well what about the other side of things, can you think of some-
             one who is considered absolutely weird.
CLIENT: Well, apart from me, I suppose Ozzy Osbourne has been pretty weird
             in his time, I guess he would rate around 80 – or anyone out of that
             family, thinking about it.
THERAPIST: Well, let's we put him on the continuum; anyone else who springs to
             mind who you would consider as being fairly weird?
CLIENT: I suppose anyone who has appeared on Jerry Springer must be fairly
             strange. Put them at about 75.

From this point the therapist can ask the individual to consider the attributes associated with Ozzy Osbourne, which in this case turned out to be behaviours such as eating live bats and other creatures. At this point, the client should be encouraged to place themselves on the continuum in relationship to the people that they have identified. This often leads to a reappraisal of their own weirdness, with an associated reduction in conviction and distress. The following case highlights the importance of core beliefs in maintaining difficulties and demonstrates the evaluation of core beliefs.

CASE EXAMPLE

Joan is a 20-year-old woman who has been attending a local college, studying A levels. She had been struggling to pass these for a number of years, and over the past year had found concentrating on her studies increasingly difficult. At the point of referral, her general concentration was extremely poor and she felt that she could not sit down for longer than five minutes to study. Her sleep pattern was very erratic, she felt depressed and socially anxious, and was becoming worried that other people were talking about her. Her diet was poor, she had lost weight and her personal hygiene was also poor. Significantly, she felt that the first goal of therapy should be to shower or bath at least once a week. She explained that she had seen a counsellor previously, although this had not been a great deal of help, and she was also seeing a counsellor at the college in order to help with study skills. She appeared to have little confidence in therapy being able to change things, and also stated that she would probably be very erratic in attendance at sessions because of her problems, apologising for this in advance. A formulation, which can be seen in Figure 11.1, was developed over the first couple of sessions alongside a problem list.

Joan wanted to pass her exams, go to university and then begin a career. Unfortunately, she had been stuck for the past few years taking her exams in order to get into university, and this was now something she felt unable to achieve.

Early on in therapy it became apparent that she had beliefs that she should be perfect. This was a dysfunctional assumption, rather than a core belief. Her core belief was that she was weird; her belief about having to be perfect was that this would prevent

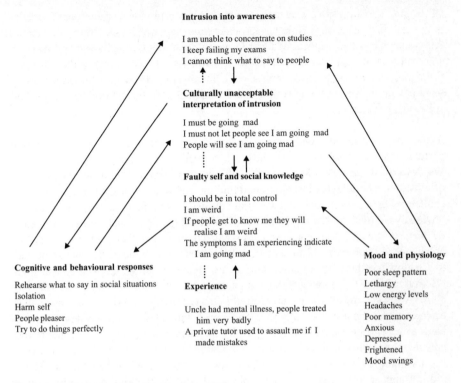

Intrusion into awareness

I am unable to concentrate on studies
I keep failing my exams
I cannot think what to say to people

**Culturally unacceptable
interpretation of intrusion**

I must be going mad
I must not let people see I am going mad
People will see I am going mad

Faulty self and social knowledge

I should be in total control
I am weird
If people get to know me they will
    realise I am weird
The symptoms I am experiencing indicate
    I am going mad

Experience

Uncle had mental illness, people treated
    him very badly
A private tutor used to assault me if I
    made mistakes

Cognitive and behavioural responses

Rehearse what to say in social situations
Isolation
Harm self
People pleaser
Try to do things perfectly

Mood and physiology

Poor sleep pattern
Lethargy
Low energy levels
Headaches
Poor memory
Anxious
Depressed
Frightened
Mood swings

Figure 11.1   Idiosyncratic case formulation

people from discovering that she was weird. Joan constantly referred to herself as weird, and she frequently referred to things that happened to her as being weird. To prevent people from seeing her as being weird she spent a great deal of energy attempting to achieve things perfectly, including social contacts and college work. She would wait for the perfect time to do things and would subsequently worry that the perfect time may never arrive.

Her beliefs about being weird stemmed from her early experiences. She had great affection for her uncle, who had a mental illness, and felt that she understood him; unfortunately, other members of the family treated her uncle very poorly and they would frequently refer to him in a derogatory manner calling him names such as 'weirdo'. Joan felt that her affinity with her uncle meant that she, herself, may be perceived as a 'weirdo'. This belief was exacerbated further when a private tutor would beat her if her work was considered to be of a poor standard. He would use words such as 'stupid' and 'weird' to describe Joan's inability to learn. It is not surprising to learn, therefore, that she developed a way of preventing not only the beatings from her tutor, but also other people from perceiving her as weird. In order to achieve this, she began to do things to a very high standard; this was obviously functional, in that it prevented further beatings from her tutor. As time went on she started to incorporate this belief into other aspects of her life, and this strategy remained functional for some time. However, when she failed her A levels this caused a great deal of distress. From this point onwards, she increased her compensatory behaviours to prevent others from perceiving her as being weird, and this appeared to be a strong trigger for her subsequent difficulties.

At the point that she attended therapy, she was very concerned with her beliefs about perfection and was achieving very little due to these beliefs hampering her progress. We developed the formulation, as shown, and this served to indicate the possible origins of this belief, which she reported finding useful. However, it was necessary to challenge her beliefs about being weird and the need for perfection. There was nothing obviously weird about Joan and she found it difficult to operationalise what she meant by the term 'weird'. However, despite this, she would frequently refer to incidents that had happened in her life, or to herself, as being weird. Such incidents were subjected to scrutiny in order to try to objectively assess their weirdness. It appeared that Joan referred to almost all incidents that happened in her life as weird. Joan was asked to clarify what she meant when she referred to herself as weird. When this was done it transpired that she was not really sure, and merely tended to use the word on a regular basis as a pejorative term that had globally negative connotations. She came to the conclusion that this may serve to sustain her belief. Joan was discouraged from using this terminology, unless there was a basis for it, after reviewing the situation. There did not appear to be any faulty perceptions of self, or anything obviously strange about her appearance or behaviour, which would have supported her beliefs.

Alongside her beliefs about being weird, we examined her beliefs about being perfect. She was quickly able to see that holding these beliefs left her vulnerable to failure and added extreme amounts of pressure. She had to contribute the perfect response in a conversation, wait for the perfect time to undertake tasks, write the perfect essay for college, and the list continued in an almost endless manner. The first of these (her contributions to conversation) was examined in detail. Joan was very fearful of engaging in social contacts because she felt unable to perform in these situations and would become extremely anxious. She would avoid social contacts if at all possible. When in a social situation she would try to think which way the conversation was going, and then think of what she could possibly contribute. She would then practise this in her mind, over and over, until she felt it was perfect. To test out the efficacy of these strategies, Joan was asked to communicate with a third person who she did not know. For the first five minutes she was to use her normal strategy, and for the second five minutes she was to drop all her compensatory strategies (or safety behaviours) and just concentrate on what was being discussed. This exercise was videotaped and the third party was also asked for feedback on how it felt to interact with Joan. This is a common strategy for working with people with social phobia (Clark, 1999). To her surprise, the third party noted that communication appeared more comfortable when

Joan did not engage in her safety behaviours, and the videotape also demonstrated to Joan that she looked more comfortable and fluent when she dropped her safety behaviours.

Time was also spent examining the pros and cons of doing things perfectly and whether some tasks were more worthy of the amount of time and energy associated with achieving them in this way. She also examined the connection between doing things perfectly and weirdness, coming to the conclusion that doing things perfectly all of the time could in itself be considered weirder than not doing things perfectly. When she considered people that she did not view as weird, she recognised that they would often make mistakes or things might go wrong for them; however, she never inferred that they were weird from this.

This approach to altering her beliefs about being weird encompassed a range of interventions. They were designed to complement each other and work together to gently challenge her beliefs about being weird. At the end of therapy she believed that she was still slightly different from others in some way, but that this was not a bad thing. She felt that her differences made her an interesting person who had alternative perspectives; however, she no longer perceived herself as weird. Joan passed her A levels and enrolled on a degree course. She had developed a wide network of social contacts and spent her time engaged in a wide range of activities, including a part-time job. These were fairly substantial improvements, considering that her initial goal of therapy had been to impact on her personal hygiene.

OTHER CORE BELIEFS

There are many core beliefs that have also been identified in people at risk of psychosis. These include beliefs about worthlessness and unlovability, beliefs about being evil, beliefs about being guilty and beliefs about helplessness. Patients in our study were also shown to score significantly higher than non-patients on fears of rejection and criticism (Morrison et al., 2002). Such beliefs are amenable to challenging using the strategies mentioned above (for more details see Padesky, 1994, or Beck, 1995). In many cases, altering these beliefs has been an important aspect of therapy; for some, the change process started without directly tackling their core beliefs, whilst for others, tackling their core beliefs has been necessary in order to enable shifts in thinking and reductions in distress. As with all aspects of the therapy process, however, these interventions should be formulation-driven.

SUMMARY

In this chapter we have examined the importance of core beliefs and how these beliefs shape the way in which people view themselves, the world and others. We have also indicated that the beliefs an individual holds (such as being weird or that the world is a dangerous place) make sense when you consider some of their early experiences. The process of identifying these beliefs in therapy is extremely important for the formulation and subsequent therapy, although modification of these beliefs may not be required. 'I am different' is a particularly common belief in people at high risk of developing psychosis. The work of Beck, Padesky and their colleagues regarding the identification and modification of core beliefs suggests numerous strategies that can be applied to evaluating core beliefs with people at risk.

12

SOCIAL ISOLATION

For many people, the onset of psychotic symptoms appears to take place when they have a reduced capacity for generating and evaluating alternative explanations for ambiguous events. Obviously, an individual can have his or her own ability to generate and evaluate such alternatives. One of the goals of CT is to help the person develop their own strategies to facilitate this process. However, no matter how effective our own strategies are, there are still occasions when we turn to others in order to assist with this process. Typically, we turn to others when things are slightly out of the ordinary, or when we feel uncertain about an event, and in doing this we move from an internal to an external facility for generating and evaluating alternative explanations. When working with individuals at risk of developing psychosis, a common factor we have observed is that, for some reason, they do not have access to external facilities for generating and evaluating such possibilities. Additionally, we have also found that, on occasion, the person they chose to turn to may actually endorse or agree with their culturally unacceptable ideas, thereby confirming their beliefs.

ACCESSING SOCIAL SUPPORT

It is apparent that, sometimes, when an individual experiences an event, which can be external to the person (e.g. someone looking at them strangely) or internal (e.g. the experience of a very unusual thought or an unusual perceptual experience), this event can lead to culturally unacceptable interpretations (as outlined in the model of psychosis). The ability to generate and evaluate alternative explanations for these experiences is an important factor in determining outcome, and this includes both external factors (e.g. having someone that the person can speak to in order to check things out) and cognitive abilities (e.g. cognitive flexibility, problem-solving and evaluation strategies). If this ability is impaired, it is possible that the stressed and vulnerable individual will start to make sense of an experience in ways that are congruent with their unhelpful beliefs, possibly leading to a psychotic misattribution of

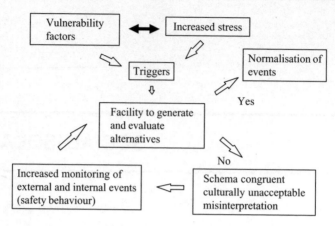

Figure 12.1   French et al.'s model of early psychotic symptoms
Source: French et al. (2001)

the initial trigger. This will lead to an increase in self-monitoring behaviour (selective attention), again directed at both external events (e.g. reading the papers more avidly to see if any news is personally directed), and internal events (e.g. increased monitoring of unusual thoughts to see if they are repeated). For a further discussion of attention and the concept of safety behaviours, see Chapter 9.

Once further threatening events are detected because of increased self-monitoring, the person may again fail to generate and evaluate alternative explanations for these experiences, potentially creating a vicious circle. Subsequently, an impaired ability to generate alternative explanations, and a reduction in external facilities for checking out possible explanations, is likely to result in an increase in culturally unacceptable interpretations (because they are not subject to social validation or scrutiny). The exit from this cycle may be via the ability to generate and evaluate alternatives, which might be facilitated by a close friend, or a cognitive-behaviour therapist who can help the individual to consider other ways of thinking, encourage better hypothesis-testing strategies, and normalise the triggering events. A heuristic diagram describing this process (from French et al., 2001) is illustrated in Figure 12.1.

Incorporating the facility to check out alternative explanations into a case conceptualisation can help to provide an account of psychosis that is acceptable to clients, is easily understood, and yet allows for a detailed cognitive exploration of symptom development. It also provides a possible explanation of why non-specific interventions such as befriending may reduce symptoms in the short term (see Sensky et al., 2000). It is also consistent with the work of Moller and Husby (2000), who found that clients experiencing their first episode reported 'reduced will' and a 'reduced ability' to disclose their initial psychotic experiences. This is certainly the case in our experience, and, as discussed earlier, many people are frightened of disclosing strange beliefs because of the consequences they imagine this would entail. People fear what will happen to them; will their disclosure lead to medicalisation of their problems, including prescription of medication or admission to hospital? Most people have some experience of psychosis, but, unfortunately, this experience is usually a negative one. They may have a friend or relative with a psychotic disorder and have seen that this person has required medication and/or admission into hospital (possibly against their will), or have seen negative portrayals of psychosis in the media. These factors combine to reduce the likelihood of someone discussing their psychotic experiences.

Examples of Loss of Social Support

The following are examples of how patients lost the ability to generate or evaluate alternatives from an external perspective.

- Someone lost contact with their peer group because they stopped taking drugs. This also led to increased contact with a high expressed emotion (EE) mother.
- Someone lost contact with the majority of their friends due to moving house. They also fell out with their new group of college friends, leaving them feeling extremely isolated.
- Someone split with their partner, which had been a long-term, and their major confiding, relationship. They felt unable to talk to family members about some of their strange cognitions due to the distressing nature of these thoughts.
- Sadly, one individual explained that they had no confiding relationships, except for a family pet that had recently died.
- Another person had recently split up with his partner, which had been a long-term relationship. This individual also tended to confide in his father; however, his father had a drug problem, which for a while was under control, but he had just started taking drugs again and his son felt unable to burden him with his own difficulties.
- One person reported that he had never felt comfortable discussing personal matters with his family. When he moved away from home and started university he did not get on with the other people on his course and felt extremely isolated.
- Someone stopped taking drugs, which meant she lost contact with her peer group. The only other major person in her life was her father and she felt unable to discuss things with him.
- One person was being bullied at work and felt very vulnerable. She had very few friends and no one she could confide in; having recently moved house exacerbated this.

- Someone returned to his home town after a period away travelling and found that his parents had moved house to another part of the country. His partner was in another country and he was living in a flat by himself in an area where there were high rates of crime. All of these combined to leave the individual feeling extremely lonely.

Examples of Other People Endorsing/Generating Odd Ideas

The following are examples of how patients have had their culturally unacceptable interpretations confirmed when attempting to check them out externally:

- Melanie was being bullied at college so she started to make friends with another girl who was considered a bit of a loner. Her new friend informed Melanie that she was a spy (code name Nikita). To prove this, Nikita showed Melanie various forms of identification with different names (representing her numerous identities), which would obviously be vital for any spy. Nikita also showed Melanie some cuts to her arms and indicated these were due to being tortured. Melanie was told that if she disclosed this information, she would be in danger, and that there were special communications networks which could pick up everything that was being said. Therefore, her conversations would be tracked in future. This prevented Melanie from asking other people's views on this matter.
- Warren felt extremely alone in the world; he had been adopted and had experienced difficulties with his adoptive parents. He met an old man who explained that certain bodily marks could indicate if you were related to the Royal Family. The old man examined Warren and told him that he was related to the Royal Family. Initially he was sceptical although as he thought about it more he remembered a time when he was younger and had shaved his head and it appeared bluish indicating 'Blue Blood' (i.e. royal connections). Warren started to believe this connection to the Royal Family and subsequently felt that members of a secret service were following him to keep an eye on him. He knew this because he spotted lots of people with shiny shoes, which he viewed as a sign of being in MI5. A friend of his endorsed this belief, telling Warren that he, too, saw lots of people with shiny shoes following Warren, and (significantly) that he also recognised that shiny shoes equated to being in MI5.
- Lara moved into a flat by herself in the centre of Manchester. When she noticed a few things happening that she had no ready explanation for she started to believe that aliens were in her flat. Her parents held strong beliefs about the existence of aliens and many people she had contact with held beliefs about the existence of spirits, aliens and other supernatural beings. When she explained these events to her parents, and people she knew, she was told that she might have some sort of gift, that she might be able to contact the spirits or be in contact with aliens. However, this caused her great distress. Significantly, when she turned to other people such as her brother or her boyfriend (both of whom lived some distance away and were,

in her terms, 'practical people') they tried to help her see alternatives to aliens or ghosts and she found this approach much less distressing.

HOW TO TACKLE THIS IN THERAPY

Highlighting the issue of isolation in the formulation is an important step. The formulation can demonstrate how the process of isolation actually maintains the problem, as would a safety behaviour (in fact, isolation can often be adopted as a safety behaviour, as discussed in Chapter 9). However, as previously discussed, fear of disclosing symptoms due to a fear of potential consequences, such as being admitted to hospital, frequently prevents disclosure. Encouraging someone to share their experiences in an experimental style can prove quite a powerful intervention.

Another method of dealing with a lack of confidant is to get the individual to list people they could turn to in order to check out some of their thoughts. This list should be exhaustive of all potential people that could act as a confidant. If the problem is that the individual has lost their usual support structure then it is important to attempt to re-initiate contact, where possible and appropriate, or to help them to generate ideas for places at which they could develop new relationships. It may be necessary to incorporate such tasks in activity scheduling, and to use role-play and video feedback to help them develop or re-learn social skills.

If the problem is that they have been turning to people who have been endorsing their beliefs, then it is necessary to explore alternative people they could turn to. If they have turned to other people, what did they say and what did they do with this information? If others had given alternatives contradicting their beliefs and they had discounted this, why had they done so?

CASE EXAMPLES

In the case of the young woman who believed in aliens/ghosts, a list was generated of all the possible people that she could talk to about her strange experiences. These people were classified into two categories: 'practical people' and 'spiritual people'. When she was alone and things happened in her flat that she found difficult to explain she would subsequently take out her list of practical people and call one of them, as opposed to the people on the spiritual list (who may well confirm or support her initial interpretation, and thus maintain her distress). This provided her with a way of choosing which strategy she should adopt in relation to how she felt. She was able to make use of all of her social networks at various times and prioritised who would be the most appropriate person to contact. This still enabled her to conceptualise many of the experiences within a framework of aliens, ghosts and spirits, and this was important because this was a strong belief she had held for many years although the result of this process was that she felt less distress associated with these experiences. If there had not been any distress, then there would obviously have been no need to carry out this intervention.

A young man, Alex, presented to his GP and explained his belief that bad things, such as nasty accidents, were going to happen to him. Also, he felt that he was able to cause unpleasant events through the power of thought, including an accident that happened to one of his close friends. Alex felt that, if this was true, then maybe he was the son of the Devil. He was frightened to discuss these experiences with his family and felt so worried that people were attempting to harm him that, at one point, he stopped eating and was drinking only water for fear of being poisoned. When he was finally taken to see his GP, he was worried that he was going to be given a lethal injection. These ideas were short-lived (approximately one week) and they resolved themselves spontaneously without the use of neuroleptic medication. The GP prescribed a course of antidepressant medication and referred Alex to the practice counsellor and also to a consultant psychiatrist.

The practice counsellor subsequently referred Alex to the local Department of Clinical Psychology and, after being assessed by one of the clinical psychologists, he was referred to our research team. He entered the study via the Brief Limited Intermittent Psychotic Symptoms (BLIPS) group, as he had experienced frank psychotic symptoms, which had resolved spontaneously after a short period of time.

There was limited evidence of psychotic ideation at the time of assessment, although Alex was very concerned about whether his BLIP would recur and wanted to understand why this had occurred in the first place. If someone has experienced these symptoms they could be vulnerable to them in the future. This possibility can set up processes of hypervigilance that may increase the likelihood of this happening again (see Gumley, White & Power, 1999). The aim of intervention with people in the BLIPS group must therefore be to facilitate their escape from this potential vicious circle.

Although Alex was experiencing minimal psychotic symptoms at the time of assessment, he was presenting as anxious, depressed, and emotionally and socially withdrawn; symptoms that have all been linked to the relapse prodrome (Birchwood et al., 1989).

The principle aim of the initial therapeutic assessment was to understand Alex's predominant concerns, which were about what had happened to him, his fear that it would happen again, and his anxiety in social situations. After assessing his recent history, it was clear that he had been under significant amounts of stress because of a number of critical events: his father's problem drinking; the death of a best friend's father (who was also a problem drinker); the ending of his relationship with a longstanding girlfriend; increased stress at work; and an attack by someone in a local club.

Problem 1	Goal statement 1
Alex was experiencing social anxiety which prevented him from going out and enjoying himself.	For Alex to be able to go out at least once per week with someone like her brother or a friend and be able to stay out for at least two hours without wanting to return home.
Problem 2	**Goal statement 2**
Alex wanted to prevent this from happening again.	We decided not to spend time on this at this point and recognised that this would be a hard goal to achieve and measure but was an understandable problem that he wanted to work on.

Figure 12.2   Problem list

Quickly reviewing these incidents, it is hardly surprising that he was experiencing stress. This observation was presented back to him as a means of normalising his distress. The assault seemed to offer a clue about the origins of his paranoid beliefs. At the end of the session Alex was given a rationale for the intervention both verbally and in written form (see Appendices for rationales for the different entry routes).

A tentative model of Alex's experiences was collaboratively discussed, and this was presented in the form of a longitudinal formulation. Time was also spent reviewing the influence of thoughts on behaviours and emotions, taking the maintenance aspect of the formulation to illustrate how the process had continued. The remainder of the session was spent developing problem statements and choosing SMART goals. This approach enables the patient and the therapist to agree targets, which they can work towards over a relatively short period of time, ensuring that the patient has success experiences. Clearly defined goals also enable the patient to break down and define his problems rather than viewing them as a mass of overwhelming difficulties, thus increasing optimism. The resulting list of prioritised problems and goals is shown in Figure 12.2.

During the following session, the main agenda item was to work on the first problem on the problem list – social anxiety and avoidance – as this was causing the most concern for Alex. The usual review of previous work was undertaken beforehand, and this revealed a recent incident, which exemplified this difficulty.

Alex had been about to go shopping and was going to catch the train to a local shopping centre. However, whilst going for the train, he met someone he knew who asked 'How are things?'; he became self-conscious, started to feel that people were watching him and this made him scan the environment for other indicators of people watching him. He became introverted and unable to discuss anything with them, and subsequently returned home due to his feelings of fear and anxiety.

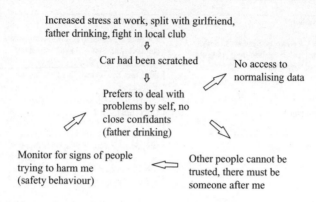

Figure 12.3 Idiosyncratic version of French et al.'s model

This incident was discussed in terms of the model. It was suggested that if Alex had had the opportunity to talk through his experiences with a sympathetic person, he would have been able to reappraise the situation and consider alternative explanations of what was happening. Alex felt very unsure what he could say to people if they asked him how he was, so the therapist worked collaboratively with him to find a suitable form of words. Role-play was then utilised until he was comfortable with his chosen way of describing his experiences, and he was able to use it in a relaxed and comfortable manner. This discussion led to the joint development of a revision to the model of early psychosis presented to Alex, which took into account his particular history and experiences. This revised model is shown in Figure 12.3.

The homework task agreed from this session was to go out and, if a similar situation arose, to try out Alex's statement about his experiences with an appropriate friend. Also, if someone who he felt comfortable talking to about his illness approached Alex, then he should do so and monitor what he or she said. As Alex had not discussed his concerns with anyone from his social circle, this had prevented him from having access to normalising data. It was hypothesised that some of his friends may have had similar experiences, or if they had not, then they would nonetheless be supportive of him. The assumption we were testing was, therefore, 'If I discuss it with people then they will think I am going mad'.

When reviewing the homework at the next session Alex found that he had only used the agreed form of words a couple of times, but that it had been available to him as a safety net had it been required. However, he had come across two other people in his close circle of friends and had disclosed some of the things he had been experiencing, and this had turned out to be highly beneficial. Interestingly, both friends had experienced some form of psychotic symptoms. One person had experienced paranoia to the point where he had wanted to move away from the area, an apparent consequence of his use of illicit drugs. Also, a close relative reported seeing a hallucination one morning upon waking, which had appeared incredibly real and frightening. These two experiences served to normalise Alex's experiences and he felt significantly more relaxed as a consequence. In the homework review, it also transpired that Alex had made significant progress towards his goal in relation to problem 1, and was now socialising more, and with less distress and concern than anticipated. He was able to stay out as long as he desired without his fears making him return home.

The agreement of this plan concluded the interventions. In five sessions he had made significant progress, to the point that he planned a trip away on holiday, was considering a change of career, and felt positive about the future. As Alex felt that his problems had been largely resolved as a consequence of the therapeutic intervention, no further sessions were planned. Alex agreed to be followed up at two-monthly intervals by a research assistant. At the two-month follow-up, Alex was not experiencing any psychotic ideation, was not emotionally or socially withdrawn and reported no symptoms of anxiety. Alex appeared quite comfortable talking to the assessor and reported going out with friends. He did report feeling a little fed up because of boredom but added that he could be easily cheered up. At four-month follow-up, Alex had changed his job and reported an active social life. At eight months all improvements had been maintained.

SUMMARY

For many people, the onset of psychotic symptoms appears to take place at a point when they have a reduced capacity for generating and evaluating alternative explanations. The process for generating and evaluating such alternatives is undertaken in two ways. The first is to do this process internally through our own cognitive skills, and the second is to seek advice from others in order to ascertain their perspective on things. It seems that, when we have ordinary experiences, we are capable of generating and evaluating alternatives using our own psychological strategies. However, if something out of the ordinary happens to us, this is the time we turn to our close confidants in order to ascertain their view on things rather than relying solely on our own capacity to process confusing information. What seems to be the case for people at high risk is that the people they would normally turn to in order to check out confusing information are either unavailable or they, in some way, endorse some of the more bizarre alternatives. In this chapter, we have identified some case examples in which individuals have either lost their usual social contacts or have approached people who have validated what could be considered more bizarre beliefs. There are several strategies that can be utilised in therapy to overcome some of these difficulties.

13

RELAPSE PREVENTION

WHY SHOULD WE UNDERTAKE RELAPSE PREVENTION?

Relapse prevention should be incorporated into any cognitive-behavioural intervention. This usually involves developing a blueprint, summarising therapeutic progress and discussion about how and when to consider accessing services in the future; each of these will be discussed in more detail. Undertaking relapse prevention is extremely important and is a routine part of the CT package when working with anxiety and depression (Fennell, 1989). However, in work developed with people with psychosis, relapse prevention can be a discreet intervention in itself (Birchwood et al., 1989; Gumley et al., 2003). For example, in Gumley and colleagues' (2003) randomised-controlled trial, 15.3% of the CBT group were admitted to hospital compared to 26.4% of the control group over 12 months, and 18.1% of the CBT group relapsed, compared with 34.7% of the control group. The relapse intervention we have adopted incorporates both of these strategies. This work is especially relevant to those patients who have experienced a BLIP, as the focus of intervention is often on preventing the recurrence of such difficulties.

The period prior to a relapse is conceptualised as the relapse prodrome, and is normally characterised by changes in the person's mood, behaviour and thoughts, which appear two to six weeks prior to relapse. In numerous illnesses there can be evidence of the onset of that illness prior to the emergence of full-blown symptoms. This often involves the emergence of sub-clinical symptoms and a range of other indicators heralding the onset of the illness.

Prodromes in psychosis appear to be typified by changes such as increased tension, eating problems, concentration problems, sleeping difficulties, depression, social withdrawal, anxiety, dysphoria and irritability (Birchwood et al., 1989). They may also include pre-psychotic signs such as suspiciousness and mild feelings of paranoia (Birchwood, 1996). The first studies that attempted to identify common signs of a prodromal phase in psychosis used a retrospective design and found that the majority of patients and their carers reported particular changes in thoughts, feelings and behaviours prior to episodes (Birchwood et al., 1989; Herz & Melville, 1980; McCandless-Glincher et al., 1986). Patients have expressed a strong interest in learning about early warning signs of their illness, and relapses, and rated it as second most important from a list of more than 40 topics (Mueser et al., 1992). It has also been found that patients tend to monitor their own symptoms and initiate responses to changes in symptoms (McCandless-Glincher et al., 1986); for example, engaging in diversionary activities, seeking professional help, and resuming or increasing medication (this is often despite a lack of guidance from services).

If these early signs and symptoms can be identified, then they may present an opportunity to act quickly in order to offer treatments aimed at minimising symptoms and the possibility of preventing subsequent relapse. Interventions in relapse prevention have generally been aimed at medication and support. However, a recent trial of CT aimed at relapse demonstrated that psychological interventions could be utilised to minimise relapse (Gumley & Power, 2000). Significantly, this study found that the most frequent thoughts reported by patients are fears of hospitalisation and the consequences of this. It is hypothesised that these thoughts trigger strong emotions, which, in turn, fuel the cognitions, and the whole process may then spiral out of control. In our work, we have found similar experiences, in that when the initial symptoms are conceptualised as indicators of impending madness, then this accelerates the very symptoms that are feared (as suggested by Gumley, White & Power, 1999).

PRACTICAL APPLICATION

Although undertaking work on relapse prevention is an important part of CT, it can sometimes prove difficult to deliver. In some cases, people will experience relief from the distress of their symptoms after a few sessions and feel no need for any further therapy. They may be keen to put their experiences behind them and get on with their lives, which is quite understandable. However, this tends to characterise a sealing-over recovery style (McGlashan, 1987), which has been associated with increased chance of relapse. A progression towards an integrating recovery style can be beneficial, as this is associated with reduced relapse rates. This information should be discussed with the client in order to allow them to make an informed decision about what they would like to do. It may also be useful to discuss 'staying well' as opposed to 'relapse prevention' as this offers a different message for the client and sells a notion of recovery as opposed to a process of repeated episodes. A rationale for this could be:

When someone has problems and they recover from them, they will frequently want to put those problems behind them. This is extremely understandable. However, if someone has experienced certain types of problems, then this indicates they are in some way vulnerable to them. One of the best ways of trying to minimise the chances of this problem recurring in the future is to learn from what happened and how you got over it, rather than pretending it did not happen. In your case, this could mean spending one or two more sessions on understanding what caused your difficulties to develop. Do you think it may be worthwhile?

Clearly, if someone does not wish to engage in relapse prevention work, this should be respected, but seeing if they will book in booster sessions in the future can be helpful. It can be explained that these are to act as a safety net in case of difficulties. This period can give the individual the opportunity to begin to test things out by themselves, without direct access to therapy. It is possible that, during this time, clients who have not fully completed a relapse component to therapy may begin to experience increased symptoms. This will give a clear rationale for undertaking relapse work and can challenge the belief that '*This is all sorted, it won't happen again*'. It is important, however, to remember that many people will not experience a relapse, regardless of undertaking relapse prevention, and their reluctance to do so should not be pathologised.

If someone has clear risk factors for vulnerability to future difficulties, then the belief that '*This will not happen again*' can be worth examining in more detail. If a person experiences the re-emergence of symptoms, then this can, as described before, trigger distress, which can lead to a vicious circle. Because many of the symptoms associated with psychosis can be part of normal experiences, their total amelioration cannot be guaranteed (nor would this be desirable). In fact, Romme and Escher (1989) would view the goal of therapy to be the liberation from the stigma of symptoms. Therefore, it is important that the individual recognises that the emergence of psychotic experiences does not necessarily herald the onset of a psychotic breakdown; rather, it is the interpretation of them, which can lead to them spiralling out of control. If the person has a belief such as, '*This may happen again, but I have some strategies to deal with it, which have been tried and tested*', then this has a less catastrophic feel to it. Therefore, relapse prevention should incorporate elements that encourage a balanced appraisal of the future emergence of symptoms, rather than a catastrophic interpretation.

THERAPEUTIC BLUEPRINT

The therapeutic blueprint consists of a written summary detailing what the patient has learnt in treatment. This should include information regarding the development and maintenance of their difficulties, including a copy of the formulation(s), strategies for evaluating beliefs, generating alternative explanations and testing them out, detailed summaries of counter evidence and the results of behavioural experiments. The patient should be encouraged to do as much of this as they can for homework, and even the gaps that are filled in with the therapist's help should be written by the patient, if possible. This will enhance ownership of the blueprint, rather than it being viewed as something the therapist thought.

We have found that this should be provided in a form which is amenable to the person (e.g. written or audiotape). However, one block to this is that many people have been extremely reluctant to have material at home, in case others were to find it. They feel that the sensitive nature of the work undertaken in therapy should remain confidential and do not want to run the risk of others seeing what has been discussed. A possible way around this, which we are hoping to develop, would be a website that the client could enter with a password, which would access their specific therapy blueprint. This would mean that the individual is not required to keep sensitive material at home, thereby preventing others from being able to see it. Unfortunately, as yet, we have been unable to make this a practical option. However, what we have found is that if people are given the opportunity to test things out, a number of them will experience a minor re-emergence of symptoms. This can be a catalyst for the individual not only to undertake relapse prevention but also an opportunity to explore the pros and cons of having information available at home relating to the process of therapy. Discussing possible hiding places and their relative security can also be advantageous.

The blueprint could also include a list of people to contact and some consideration of at what point they should seek help again (if their symptoms become unmanageable). This could include friends or family members in the initial stages, therapists, phone numbers of help lines, GP contact details and the details of any other people the client has found to be of help. When these people should be contacted should be operationalised in terms of frequency and severity of symptoms and a final point could be attendance at a local casualty department or crisis team, should things become so distressing that they require emergency assistance.

SUMMARY

Undertaking relapse prevention should be seen as an important aspect of therapy and, in CT the use of a blueprint summarising the work that has been undertaken is common practice. In working with psychotic patients, relapse prevention can also be delivered as a discreet intervention by itself if that is all the client wishes to engage with. Relapse prevention initiatives aim to identify warning signs, possibly signalling the re-emergence of symptoms and allowing interventions to be delivered in the early stages in an effort to prevent the escalation of these sub-clinical symptoms into a full-blown episode. One of the difficulties associated with this intervention is that it is based on the concept of the prodrome, which is a retrospective one. Therefore, times may arise when warning signs appear that would not lead to a psychotic episode (i.e. they are false positives). However, having the ability to intervene at the earliest point in the development of symptoms, whether they evolve or not, is something that many people find appealing (if not at first, then after subsequent episodes, should they occur).

Targeting appraisals relating to the re-emergence of symptoms is important. Many people believe that things will never happen to them again and relate their symptoms to a complex series of events, which could never be repeated. However, as described throughout this book, many of the symptoms experienced can be perceived as normal experiences and it is their appraisal as being *ab*normal that leads to distress. If the individual believes that these experiences are never going to recur, and then they do, then this can lead to distress; it is therefore important for people not to catastrophically interpret the emergence of such experiences. The process of relapse prevention should target these beliefs and provide written summaries of strategies undertaken throughout therapy.

14

CONCLUSIONS

The onset of psychosis has devastating consequences for millions of people world-wide. The majority of mental health budgets go towards the treatment of people with psychotic disorders, primarily because inpatient beds are usually filled with individuals who experience psychosis. The length of stay in these beds can be significant; even when someone is considered ready for discharge, there can be delays resulting from difficulties in establishing packages of care to provide support in the community. There is considerable stigma associated with psychosis and many people wish to avoid talking about their experiences because of fears regarding how others will perceive them.

Even the newer antipsychotic medications have a range of unpleasant and, for some, disabling side effects. For many years, the focus of treatment for psychosis has been about how we can limit symptoms, since the Kraepelinian model, which has traditionally predominated, emphasised a degenerative brain disease associated with inevitable decline. The move towards early intervention strategies has challenged this conceptualisation and has led to the concept of primary prevention.

The prevention of psychosis is attracting increasing interest; however, there are a number of concerns associated with this approach. A central component of this intervention relies upon the ability to accurately identify high-risk groups. Critics of preventative approaches to psychosis argue that identifying people as being at risk, when some of these will never develop a psychotic disorder (the false positives), is a major problem. However, there is a growing body of research which indicates that the ability to accurately predict risk is improving. A number of studies have been undertaken around the world which have demonstrated that it is possible to identify high-risk populations in which a sizable proportion of people will develop psychosis in the near future. However, there are clearly ethical considerations that need to be addressed. These include the types of intervention that could be employed, whether to intervene at all, the language and terminology that is used to describe the high-risk population, and the right of people who are at risk not to know. It is likely that the ethical debate regarding what kinds of interventions are acceptable to people at high risk, and the terminology that is appropriate, will continue for some time.

Cognitive interventions employed for the primary prevention of psychosis are an exciting development. Such interventions will, hopefully, minimise the risk of harmful side effects and can be useful to people identified as being at risk who will not develop psychosis. This approach also challenges the medical model of psychosis, which assumes psychosis (and, more specifically, schizophrenia) is the result of a brain disease or inherent genetic vulnerability. Clearly, there are some biological changes associated with the development of psychosis; indeed, some changes have been noted in the neuroanatomy of people at high risk of psychosis (Pantelis et al., 2003). However, as in depression or panic disorder, where biological changes can be detected, their existence does not necessarily imply causation; rather, this could be a result of the disorder or another process. [For example, Read et al. (2001) have suggested that childhood trauma may cause both neurological changes and unusual experiences.] It is particularly important, when working with a high-risk population, to keep an open mind about the causes of psychosis, and to be optimistic and recovery-focused.

FURTHER TRAINING AND SKILLS DEVELOPMENT

In order to practise CT, it is essential that practitioners have access to regular clinical supervision from experienced and qualified supervisors. Anyone embarking upon the provision of CT to people at high risk of developing psychosis should have experience of CT with people with psychosis and of CT with anxiety disorders, depression and other common emotional disorders. It is evident that there is considerable overlap in the difficulties experienced by people at risk of developing psychosis and those faced by patients with emotional disorders. Indeed, the problem lists of our clients typically involve difficulties such as panic attacks, post-traumatic stress disorder (PTSD), social phobia, depression, worry, low self-esteem and intrusive thoughts. Therefore, it is important that people delivering CT to people at risk of psychosis are familiar with the relevant models for these disorders (e.g. Beck, 1976; Clark, 1986; Clark & Wells, 1995; Ehlers & Clark, 2000; Fennell, 1997; Salkovskis, 1985; Wells, 1995) and the treatment strategies derived from them. It is also important that therapists are familiar with strategies for changing core beliefs, such as those described by Padesky (1994) and Beck (1995). Maintaining these skills is also important, and ongoing training and keeping up-to-date with new developments in the fields of psychosis and emotional disorders are strongly recommended. It is important to utilise the structure and process of CT (e.g. setting agendas, developing shared problem lists and goals and formulations in the first few sessions, setting homework and encouraging clients to listen to session tapes) to promote engagement, rather than adopting a supportive, non-specific stance.

FUTURE DIRECTIONS

There are several developments that may occur over the next few years. Given that early intervention, including early detection and preventative treatment, is a high priority within the Department of Health's strategy for delivering mental health care, it is likely that there will be a large amount of research and clinical development in relation to such topics. An important aspect of future research and development will be epidemiological studies that examine the representativeness of people at high risk (i.e. what proportion of first episodes of psychosis would have met PACE criteria prior to their episode) and the prevalence of people meeting high-risk criteria in the general population.

It would seem likely that CT for people at high risk will evolve and become more effective. The development of a group format for the delivery of CT may be a useful addition or alternative to individual CT. The diversity of problems and goals that are identified by such patients may be problematic for such an approach; however, there are several common themes that seem to recur, and a group format would be advantageous for the purposes of normalisation of people's experiences and distress, and for the development of age-appropriate social contacts. It may also be possible to involve service users or ex-service users in the delivery of such groups, which may prove useful for engaging patients who are, understandably, reluctant to trust mental health services. Involving service users in decisions regarding terminology and the ethics of early detection will also be a welcome, and hopefully productive, step.

It may be possible to further refine the criteria for identifying people at high risk of developing psychosis, possibly utilising psychological and social factors that have been discussed within this book. For example, combining cut-off scores on measures of schizotypal experiences, metacognitive beliefs or use of safety behaviours, with the PACE criteria for at-risk mental states, may increase specificity. Similarly, using past or current social circumstances, such as a history of childhood physical or sexual abuse, or current social isolation, in combination with the PACE criteria may also be helpful.

It may also be possible to learn more about the early course of psychotic disorders from studying this group of people. This may be useful for developing phase-specific treatment strategies and may also help to identify resilience factors that may prevent people from making transition to psychosis. Over time, we may also be able to develop specific protocols for CT for each of the subgroups (e.g. people with attenuated symptoms, people with a first-degree relative with psychosis and people who have experienced a BLIP).

The possibility of preventing psychosis using a psychological approach is clearly an exciting one, and it is hoped that this book will serve to encourage others to implement and develop such strategies with their local population.

APPENDICES

APPENDICES

APPENDIX 1

CLIENT-FRIENDLY FORMULATION

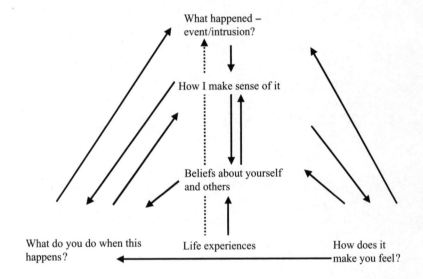

APPENDIX 1

CLIENT-FRIENDLY FORMULATION

APPENDIX 2

FORM FOR GENERATING ALTERNATIVES

GENERATING ALTERNATIVES

Name: Date:

Intrusive thought identified	
Current explanation for thought; belief rating	
Current mood associated with this belief	

It can be helpful if we look at all of the possible explanations for this thought. I am aware that you have indicated the belief above as being the main reason for this although if there are any other alternatives for this I would be very keen to understand them.

Explanation for intrusion	Belief rating (1–100) 1 = this is not the reason I am having this thought 100 = this is definitely the reason I am having this thought	Associated mood

APPENDIX 3

EXPERIMENT SHEET

Experiment sheet

Thought to be tested:

Belief in thought: (0–100%)   *Before experiment:*   *After experiment:*

Experiment to test thought	Likely problems	Strategies to deal with problems	Expected outcome	Actual outcome	Alternative thought

APPENDIX 4

WEEKLY ACTIVITY SHEET

	Monday	Tuesday	Wednesday	Thursday	Friday	Saturday	Sunday
9–10							
10–11							
11–12							
12–1							
1–2							
2–3							
3–4							
4–5							
5–6							
6–7							
7–8							
8–12							

M for Mastery, 1 = Very poor, 10 = Very good, P for Pleasure, 1 = Very poor, 10 = Very good

CLIENT-TREATMENT RATIONALE

BLIPS GROUP RATIONALE

At some point in the recent past you will have experienced some odd thoughts, perceived things slightly differently or maybe heard things such as noises or voices, even when there was no one around. These things may have caused you some distress, or may even have led to people around you becoming concerned about you.

Around this time you may have been under more than usual amounts of stress for various reasons and this could have affected things like sleep; you might have started drinking more than usual or even taking drugs.

In combination, reduced sleep and increased stress can lead to people having 'odd thoughts' which would be out of keeping with the way they generally think about things.

These strange experiences will have gone and you will possibly not want to talk about them much, perhaps out of fear that they may return or because they were so upsetting that you just want to forget about them. It may be the case that these things never come back again and you will be fine. However, there is also a possibility that, in the future, if you are in a similar position with increased amounts of stress that you may react in a similar way.

What we feel is that by tackling these difficulties rather than leaving them, we can work to prevent any further difficulties in the future, or certainly to minimise the potential of them happening in the future. The way we propose to do this is through a talking form of therapy that will look at the way you think about things and how these thoughts impact upon what you do and how you feel.

CLIENT-TREATMENT RATIONALE

ATTENUATED SYMPTOMS GROUP RATIONALE

You have been referred to our team due to some difficulties you may be experiencing with the way you think, perceive things or may be hearing strange things, such as noise or voices. These things will not be happening that frequently and in fact some of the time you may be able to ignore them or do things which stop or minimise these experiences. However, there has been sufficient concern, either from yourself or someone close to you, that some assistance from our team may be of benefit.

Around this time you may have been under more than usual amounts of stress for various reasons and this could have affected things like sleep; you might have started drinking more than usual or even taking drugs.

In combination, reduced sleep and increased stress can lead to people having 'odd thoughts' which would be out of keeping with the way they generally think about things.

You may well think that these experiences are not that bad and not worth bothering talking about, you may feel unsure about what they are but not feel particularly distressed; on the other hand they could be affecting some aspects of the way you usually live your life.

It could well be that things resolve themselves over a period of time, that things return to normal and you do not have anything like this happen again in the future. However, there is another possibility that if things continue they could potentially get worse. We cannot say at this point which group you fit into.

What we feel is that by tackling these difficulties at this point, rather than just leaving them, we could help to resolve them early and also work towards preventing them happening again, or minimising the potential for them happening again. The way we propose to do this is through a talking form of therapy that will look at the way you think about things and how these thoughts impact upon what you do and how you feel.

CLIENT-TREATMENT RATIONALE

FAMILY GROUP RATIONALE

You have been referred to our team because you will have been experiencing some difficulties recently and most likely experiencing more stress than usual. This may well have affected your general health or mental health to the point that you are experiencing some difficulties but somehow uncertain about what is happening. You will have a close family member who has had some mental health problems in the past and this may well increase personal fears about what is happening to you.

You may feel worried about sharing these fears for many reasons. It may be that the person in your family has been extremely poorly and spent long periods of time in hospital, there may be more than one family member with mental health problems and your fears could surround this happening to you.

Frequently, when people have worries, these affect things like their sleep and eating patterns. In combination, reduced sleep and increased stress can lead to people having 'odd thoughts' which would be out of keeping with the way they generally think about things.

You may not want anything to do with services, and this could be in light of your relatives' experiences. It may be that you hope your problem will resolve itself and go away, and that is exactly what might happen. However, another possibility is that things could get worse over a period of time.

What we feel is that by tackling these difficulties at this point, rather than just leaving them, we could help to resolve them early and also work towards preventing them happening again, or minimising the potential for them happening again. The way we propose to do this is through a talking form of therapy, which will look at the way you think about things, and how these thoughts impact upon what you do and how you feel.

PRIMARY CARE GUIDELINES FOR IDENTIFICATION OF SUSPECTED OR FIRST-EPISODE PSYCHOSIS

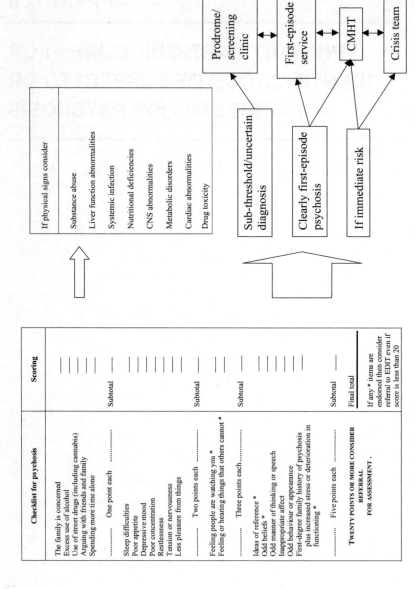

Checklist for psychosis

	Scoring
The family is concerned	———
Excess use of alcohol	———
Use of street drugs (including cannabis)	———
Arguing with friends and family	———
Spending more time alone	———
One point each Subtotal	——
Sleep difficulties	———
Poor appetite	———
Depressive mood	———
Poor concentration	———
Restlessness	———
Tension or nervousness	———
Less pleasure from things	———
Feeling people are watching you *	———
Feeling or hearing things that others cannot *	———
Two points each Subtotal	——
Three points each Subtotal	——
Ideas of reference *	———
Odd beliefs *	———
Odd manner of thinking or speech	———
Inappropriate affect	———
Odd behaviour or appearance	———
First-degree family history of psychosis plus increased stress or deterioration in functioning *	———
Five points each Subtotal	——
	Final total ——
TWENTY POINTS OR MORE CONSIDER REFERRAL FOR ASSESSMENT .	If any * items are endorsed then consider referral to EDIT even if score is less than 20

If physical signs consider

Substance abuse
Liver function abnormalities
Systemic infection
Nutritional deficiencies
CNS abnormalities
Metabolic disorders
Cardiac abnormalities
Drug toxicity

Sub-threshold/uncertain diagnosis → Prodrome/screening clinic ↔ First-episode service ↔ CMHT ↔ Crisis team

Clearly first-episode psychosis →

If immediate risk →

Source: adapted from Launer & MacKean (2000)

REFERENCES

American Psychiatric Association (1994). *Diagnostic and Statistical Manual of Mental Disorders (DSM) Fourth Edition*. APA: Washington DC.

Baker, C. & Morrison, A. P. (1998). Metacognition, intrusive thoughts and auditory hallucinations. *Psychological Medicine, 28*, 1199–1208.

Barnes, T. R. E., Hutton, S. B., Chapman, M. J. et al. (2000). West London first episode study of schizophrenia: clinical correlates of duration of untreated psychosis. *British Journal of Psychiatry, 177*, 207–211.

Beck, A. T. (1952). Successful outpatient psychotherapy of a chronic schizophrenic with a delusion based on borrowed guilt. *Psychiatry, 15*, 305–312.

Beck, A. T. (1976). *Cognitive Therapy and the Emotional Disorders*. New York: International Universities Press.

Beck, A. T., Rush, A. J., Shaw, B. F. & Emery, G. (1979). *Cognitive Therapy of Depression*. New York: Guilford Press.

Beck, A. T., Epstein, N., Harrison, R. P. & Emery, G. (1983). *Development of the Sociotropy-autonomy Scale: A measure of personality factors in psychopathology*. Unpublished manuscript, Centre for Cognitive Therapy, University of Pennsylvania Medical School, Philadelphia.

Beck, J. S. (1995). *Cognitive Therapy: Basics and Beyond*. New York: Guilford Press.

Beiser, M., Erikson, D., Fleming, J. A. & Iacono, W. G. (1993). Establishing the onset of psychotic illness. *American Journal of Psychiatry, 150*, 1349–1354.

Bell, M., Milstein, R., Beam-Goulet, J., Lysaker, P. & Cicchetti, D. (1992). The positive and negative syndrome scale and the Brief Psychiatric Rating Scale: reliability, comparability and predictive validity. *Journal of Nervous and Mental Disease, 180*, 723–728.

Bentall, R. P. (1990). *Reconstructing Schizophrenia*. London: Routledge.

Bentall, R. P. & Kaney, S. (1996). Abnormalities of self representation and persecutory delusions. *Psychological Medicine, 26*, 1231–1237.

Bentall, R. P. & Morrison, A. P. (2002). More harm than good: the case against using antipsychotic drugs to prevent severe mental illness. *Journal of Mental Health, 11*, 351–365.

Bentall, R. P., Claridge, G. S. & Slade, P. D. (1989). The multidimensional nature of schizotypal traits: a factor analytic study with normal subjects. *British Journal of Clinical Psychology, 28*, 363–375.

Bentall, R. P., Kinderman, P. & Kaney, S. (1994). The self, attributional processes and abnormal beliefs: towards a model of persecutory delusions. *Behaviour Research and Therapy, 32*, 331–341.

Birchwood, M. J. (1996). Early intervention in psychotic relapse: cognitive approaches to detection and management. In G. Haddock & P. D. Slade (eds), *Cognitive Behavioural Interventions with Psychotic Disorders*. London: Routledge.

Birchwood, M. & Chadwick, P. (1997). The omnipotence of voices: testing the validity of a cognitive model. *Psychological Medicine, 27*, 1345–1353.

Birchwood, M. J. & MacMillan, F. (1993). Early intervention in schizophrenia. *Australian and New Zealand Journal of Psychiatry, 27*, 374–378.

Birchwood, M., Todd, P. & Jackson, C. (1998). Early intervention in psychosis: the critical period hypothesis. *British Journal of Psychiatry (supplement), 172*(33), 53–59.

Birchwood, M. J., Smith, J., MacMillan, F. et al. (1989). Predicting relapse in schizophrenia: the development and implementation of an early signs monitoring system using patients and families as observers. *Psychological Medicine, 19*, 649–656.

Cartwright-Hatton, S. & Wells, A. (1997). Beliefs about worry and intrusions: the metacognitions questionnaire and its correlates. *Journal of Anxiety Disorders, 11*, 279–296.

Chadwick, P. & Birchwood, M. (1994). The omnipotence of voices: a cognitive approach to auditory hallucinations. *British Journal of Psychiatry, 164*, 190–201.

Chadwick, P. D. & Lowe, C. F. (1990). Measurement and modification of delusional beliefs. *Journal of Consulting and Clinical Psychology, 58*, 225–232.

Chadwick, P., Birchwood, M. & Trower, P. (1996). *Cognitive Therapy for Voices, Delusions and Paranoia*. New York: John Wiley & Sons.

Claridge, G., McCreery, C., Mason, O. et al. (1996). The factor structure of 'schizotypal' traits: a large replication study. *British Journal of Clinical Psychology, 35*, 103–115.

Clark, D. M. (1986). A cognitive approach to panic disorder. *Behaviour Research and Therapy, 24*, 461–470.

Clark, D. M. (1996). Panic disorder: from theory to therapy. In P. M. Salkovskis (ed.), *Frontiers of Cognitive Therapy*. New York: Guilford Press.

Clark, D. M. (1999). Anxiety disorders: why they persist and how to treat them. *Behaviour Research and Therapy (supplement), 37*, 5–27.

Clark, D. M. & Wells, A. (1995). A cognitive model of social phobia. In R. G. Heimberg & M. R. Liebowitz (eds), *Social Phobia: Diagnosis, Assessment, and Treatment* (pp. 69–93). New York: Guilford Press.

Crow, T. J., Macmillan, J. F., Johnson, A. L. & Johnstone, E. (1986). The Northwick Park study of first episodes of schizophrenia: II. A randomised controlled trial of prophylactic neuroleptic treatment. *British Journal of Psychiatry, 148*, 120–127.

Department of Health (2000). *The NHS Plan: A Plan for Investment, a Plan for Reform*. London: The Stationery Office.

Department of Health (2001). *The Mental Health Policy Implementation Guide*. London: DoH.

Drake, R. J., Haley, C. J., Akhtar, S. & Lewis, S. W. (2000). Causes of duration of untreated psychosis in schizophrenia. *British Journal of Psychiatry, 177*, 511–515.

Drury, V., Birchwood, M., Cochrane, R. & Macmillan, F. (1996). Cognitive therapy and recovery from acute psychosis: a controlled trial. I: impact on psychotic symptoms. *British Journal of Psychiatry, 169*, 593–601.

Ehlers, A. & Clark, D. M. (2000). A cognitive model of posttraumatic stress disorder. *Behaviour Research and Therapy, 38*(4), 319–345.

Fadden, G. (1997). Behavioural family therapy approaches to the treatment of schizophrenia. In C. Mace & F. Margison (eds), *Psychotherapy of Psychosis*. London: Gaskell.

Falloon, I. R. H. (1992). Early intervention for first episodes of schizophrenia: a preliminary exploration. *Psychiatry, 55*, 4–15.

Fear, C., Sharp, H. & Healy, D. (1996). Cognitive processes in delusional disorders. *British Journal of Psychiatry, 168*, 61–67.

Fennell, M. J. V. (1989). Depression. In K. Hawton, P. M. Salkovskis, J. Kirk & D. M. Clark (eds), *Cognitive Behaviour Therapy for Psychiatric Problems: A Practical Guide*. Oxford: Oxford University Press.

Fennell, M. J. V. (1997). Low self-esteem: a cognitive perspective. *Behavioural and Cognitive Psychotherapy, 25*, 1–26.

Fowler, D., Garety, P. A. & Kuipers, L. (1995). *Cognitive Behaviour Therapy for Psychosis: Theory and Practice.* Chichester: John Wiley & Sons.

Frame, L. & Morrison, A. P. (2001). Causes of PTSD in psychosis. *Archives of General Psychiatry, 58*, 305–306.

Freeman, D. & Garety, P. A. (1999). Worry, worry processes and dimensions of delusions: an exploratory investigation of a role for anxiety processes in the maintenance of delusional distress. *Behavioural and Cognitive Psychotherapy, 27*, 47–62.

French, P., Morrison, A. P., Walford, L., Knight, A. & Bentall, R. P. (2001). Cognitive therapy for preventing transition to psychosis in high-risk individuals: a single case study. In A. P. Morrison (ed.), *A Case Book of Cognitive Therapy for Psychosis.* London: Brunner Routledge.

French, P., Morrison, A. P., Walford, L., Knight, A. & Bentall, R. P. (2003). Cognitive therapy for preventing transition to psychosis in high risk individuals: a case series. *Behavioural and Cognitive Psychotherapy, 31*, 53–67.

Garety, P. A., Kuipers, E., Fowler, D., Freeman, D. & Bebbington, P. (2001). A cognitive model of the positive symptoms of psychosis. *Psychological Medicine, 31*(2), 189–195.

Gleeson, J., Larsen, T. K. & McGorry, P. (2003). Psychological treatments in pre and early psychosis. *Journal of the American Acadamy of Psychoanalyasis and Dynamic Psychiatry, 31*(1), 229–245.

Goldberg, D. P. & Hillier, V. F. (1979). A scaled version of the General Health Questionnaire. *Psychological Medicine, 9*(2), 337–353.

Gottesman, I. I. (1991). *Schizophrenia Genesis: The Origins of Madness.* San Francisco, USA: Freeman.

Gottesman, L. & Erlenmeyer-Kimling (2001). Family and twin strategies as a head start in defining prodromes and endophenotypes for hypothetical early-interventions in schizophrenia. *Schizophrenia Research, 51*, 93–102.

Gottesman, I. I. & Shields, J. (1982). *Schizophrenia: The Epigenetic Puzzle.* Cambridge: Cambridge University Press.

Greenberger, D. & Padesky, C. A. (1995). *Mind Over Mood.* New York: Guilford Press.

Grimby, A. (1993). Bereavement among elderly people: grief reactions, post-bereavement hallucinations and quality of life. *Acta Psychiatrica Scandinavica, 87*, 72–80.

Gross, G., Huber, G., Klosterkotter, J. & Linz, M. (1989). *Bonner Skala fur die Beurteilung von Basissymptomen.* Berlin/Heidelberg/New York: Springer Verlag.

Gumley, A. I. & Power, K. G. (2000). Is targeting cognitive therapy during relapse in psychosis feasible. *Behavioural and Cognitive Psychotherapy, 28*(2), 161–174.

Gumley, A., White, C. A. & Power, K. (1999). An interacting cognitive subsystems model of relapse and the course of psychosis. *Clinical Psychology and Psychotherapy, 6*, 261–278.

Gumley, A., O'Grady, M., McNay, L., Reilly, J. & Norrie, J. (2003). Early intervention for relapse in schizophrenia: results of a 12-month randomised controlled trial of cognitive behavioural therapy. *Psychological Medicine, 33*(3), 419–431.

Hafner, H., Maurer, K., Loffler, W. et al. (1994). The epidemiology of early schizophrenia. Influence of age and gender on onset and early course. *British Journal of Psychiatry (supplement), 23*, 29–38.

Halpin, S. A. & Carr, V. J. (2000). Use of quantitative rating scales to assess outcome in schizophrenia prevention studies. *Australian and New Zealand Journal of Psychiatry (supplement), 34*, S150–S160.

Hawton, K. & Kirk, J. (1989). Problem-solving. In K. Hawton, P. M. Salkovskis, J. Kirk & D. M. Clark (eds), *Cognitive Behavioural Therapy for Psychiatric Problems: A Practical Guide.* Oxford: Oxford University Press.

Herz, M. & Melville, C. (1980). Relapse in schizophrenia. *American Journal of Psychiatry, 137*, 801–812.

Hollon, S. D., DeRubeis, R. J. & Evans, M. D. (1996). Cognitive therapy in the treatment and prevention of depression. In P. M. Salkovskis (ed.), *Frontiers of Cognitive Therapy*. New York: Guilford Press.

Huber, G., Gross, G., Schuttler, R. & Linz, M. (1980). Longitudinal studies of schizophrenic patients. *Schizophrenia Bulletin, 6*, 592–605.

Jablensky, A., Sartorius, N., Ernberg, G. et al. (1992). Schizophrenia: manifestations, incidence and course in different cultures: a World Health Organisation ten-country study. *Psychological Medicine Monograph (supplement), 20*, 1–97.

Johnstone, E. C., Crow, T. J., Johnson, A. L. & MacMillan, J. F. (1986). The Northwick Park study of first episode schizophrenia: I, presentations of the illness and problems relating to admission. *British Journal of Psychiatry, 148*, 115–120.

Kay, S. R., Fiszbein, A. & Opler, L. A. (1987). The Positive and Negative Syndrome Scale (PANSS) for schizophrenia. *Schizophrenia Bulletin, 13*, 261–276.

Kay, S. R., Opler, L. A. & Lindenmayer, J. (1988). Reliability and validity of the positive and negative syndrome scale for schizophrenia. *Psychiatry Research, 23*, 99–110.

Kinderman, P. & Cooke, A. (eds) (2000). *Understanding Mental Illness: Recent Advances in Understanding Mental Illness and Psychotic Experiences*. London: British Psychological Society Division of Clinical Psychology.

Kingdon, D. G. & Turkington, D. (1994). *Cognitive Behavioural Therapy of Schizophrenia*. New York: Guilford Press.

Kirk, J. (1989). Cognitive-behavioural assessment. In K. Hawton, P. M. Salkovskis, J. Kirk & D. M. Clark (eds), *Cognitive Behavioural Therapy for Psychiatric Problems: A Practical Guide*. Oxford: Oxford University Press.

Klosterkoetter, J., Hellmich, M., Steinmeyer, E. M. & Schultze-Lutter, F. (2001). Diagnosing schizophrenia in the initial prodromal phase. *Archives of General Psychiatry, 58*, 158–164.

Kuipers, E., Garety, P., Fowler, D. et al. (1997). London-East Anglia randomised controlled trial of cognitive-behavioural therapy for psychosis, I: effects of the treatment phase. *British Journal of Psychiatry, 171*, 319–327.

Larsen, T. K., Bechdolf, A. & Birchwood, M. (2003). The concept of schizophrenia and phase-specific treatment: cognitive-behavioral treatment in pre-psychosis and in nonresponders. *Journal of the American Academy of Psychoanalysis and Dynamic Psychiatry, 31*(1), 209–228.

Launer, M. & MacKean, W. (2000). Effective management of schizophrenia within primary care. *Progress in Neurology and Psychiatry, 4*(1), 24–27.

Liddle, P. F. (1987). The symptoms of chronic schizophrenia: a re-examination of the positive-negative dichotomy. *British Journal of Psychiatry, 151*, 145–151.

Liese, B. S. & Franz, R. A. (1996). Treating substance use disorders with cognitive therapy. In P. M. Salkovskis (ed.), *Frontiers of Cognitive Therapy*. London: Guilford Press.

Loebel, A. D., Lieberman, J. A., Alvir, J. M. J. et al. (1992). Duration of psychosis and outcome in first episode schizophrenia. *American Journal of Psychiatry, 149*, 1183–1188.

McCandless-Glincher, L., Mcknight, S., Hamera, E. et al. (1986). Use of symptoms by schizophrenics to monitor and regulate their illness. *Hospital and Community Psychiatry, 37*, 929–933.

McGlashan, T. H. (1987). Recovery style from mental illness and long term outcome. *Journal of Nervous and Mental Disease, 175*, 681–685.

McGlashan, T. H., Zipursky, R. B., Perkins, D. et al. (2003). The PRIME North America randomized double-bind clinical trial of olanzapine versus placebo in patients at risk of being prodromally symptomatic for psychosis. I. Study rationale and design. *Schizophrenia Research, 61*, 7–18.

McGorry, P. D. (1995). A treatment relevant classification of psychotic disorders. *Australian and New Zealand Journal of Psychiatry, 26*, 3–17.

McGorry, P. D., Chanen, A., McCarthy, E. et al (1991). Posttraumatic stress disorder following recent-onset psychosis: an unrecognized postpsychotic syndrome. *Journal of Nervous and Mental Disease, 179*, 253–258.

McGorry, P. D., Edwards, J., Mihalopoulos, C., Harrigan, S. M. & Jackson, H. J. (1996). EPPIC: an evolving system of early detection and optimal management. *Schizophrenia Bulletin, 22*(2), 305–326.

McGorry, P. D., Yung, A. R., Phillips, L. J. et al. (2002). Randomized controlled trial of interventions designed to reduce the risk of progression to first episode psychosis in a clinical sample with subthreshold symptoms. *Archives of General Psychiatry, 59*, 921–928.

Mason, O., Claridge, G. S. & Jackson, M. (1995). New scales for the measurement of schizotypy. *Personality and Individual Differences, 18*, 7–13.

May, R. (2000). Routes to recovery from psychosis: the roots of a clinical psychologist. *Clinical Psychology Forum, 146*, 6–10.

Miller, L. J., O'Connor, E. & DiPasquale, T. (1993). Patients' attitudes towards hallucinations. *American Journal of Psychiatry, 150*, 289–588.

Miller, T. J. & McGlashan, T. H. (2000). Early identification and intervention in psychotic illness. *American Journal of Psychiatry, 157*(7), 1041–1050.

Miller, T. J., McGlashan, T. H., Woods, S. W. et al. (1999). Symptom assessment in schizophrenic prodromal states. *Psychiatric Quarterly, 70*, 273–287.

Moller, P. & Husby, R. (2000). The initial prodrome in schizophrenia: searching for naturalistic core dimensions of experience and behaviour. *Schizophrenia Bulletin, 26*(1), 217–232.

Morrison, A. P. (1998a). A cognitive analysis of the maintenance of auditory hallucinations: are voices to schizophrenia what bodily sensations are to panic? *Behavioural and Cognitive Psychotherapy, 26*(4), 289–302.

Morrison, A. P. (1998b). Cognitive behaviour therapy for psychotic symptoms in schizophrenia. In N. Tarrier, A. Wells & G. Haddock (eds), *Treating Complex Cases: The Cognitive-behavioural Therapy Approach*. Chichester: John Wiley & Sons.

Morrison, A. P. (2001). The interpretation of intrusions in psychosis: an integrative cognitive approach to hallucinations and delusions. *Behavioural and Cognitive Psychotherapy, 29*, 257–276.

Morrison, A. P. & Baker, C. A. (2000). Intrusive thoughts and auditory hallucinations: a comparative study of intrusions in psychosis. *Behaviour Research and Therapy, 38*, 1097–1106.

Morrison, A. P., Haddock, G. & Tarrier, N. (1995). Intrusive thoughts and auditory hallucinations: a cognitive approach. *Behavioural and Cognitive Psychotherapy, 23*, 265–280.

Morrison, A. P., Wells, A. & Nothard, S. (2000). Cognitive factors in predisposition to auditory and visual hallucinations. *British Journal of Clinical Psychology, 39*, 67–78.

Morrison, A. P., Wells, A. & Nothard, S. (2002). Cognitive and emotional factors as predictors of predisposition to hallucinations. *British Journal of Clinical Psychology, 41*, 259–270.

Morrison, A. P., Bentall, R. P., French, P. et al. (2002). A randomised controlled trial of early detection and cognitive therapy for preventing transition to psychosis in high risk individuals: study design and interim analysis of transition rate and psychological risk factors. *British Journal of Psychiatry, 181 (supplement 43)*, 78–84.

Morrison, A. P., Renton, J., Dunn, H., Williams, S. & Bentall, R. P. (2003). *Cognitive Therapy for Psychosis: A Formulation-based Approach*. London: Psychology Press.

Mrazek, P. J. & Haggerty, R. J. (eds) (1994). *Reducing Risks for Mental Disorders: Frontiers for Preventative Intervention Research*. Washington, DC, USA: National Academy Press.

Mueser, K. T., Bellack, A. S., Wade, J. H., Sayers, S. L. & Rosenthal, C. K. (1992). An assessment of the educational needs of chronic psychiatric patients and their relatives. *British Journal of Psychiatry, 160*, 674–680.

Neuchterlein, K. H. & Dawson, M. (1984). A heuristic vulnerability stress model of schizophrenic episodes. *Schizophrenia Bulletin, 10*, 300–312.

Norman, R. M. G. & Malla, A. K. (2001). Duration of untreated psychosis: a critical examination of the concept and its importance. *Psychological Medicine, 31*, 381–400.

Overall, J. E. & Gorham, D. R. (1962). The Brief Psychiatric Rating Scale. *Psychological Reports, 10*, 799–812.

Padesky, C. A. (1994). Schema change processes in cognitive therapy. *Clinical Psychology and Psychotherapy, 1*, 267–278.

Pantelis, C., Velakoulis, D., McGorry, P. D. et al. (2003). Neuroanatomical abnormalities before and after onset of psychosis: a cross sectional and longitudinal MRI comparison. *Lancet, 361*, 281–288.

Pelosi, A. J. & Birchwood, M. (2003). Is early intervention for psychosis a valuable waste of resources? *British Journal of Psychiatry, 182*, 196–198.

Peters, E. R., Joseph, S. A. & Garety, P. A. (1999). Measurement of delusional ideation in the normal population: introducing the PDI (Peters et al. Delusions Inventory). *Schizophrenia Bulletin, 25*(3), 553–576.

Pharoah, F., Mari, J. & Striener, D. (2000). Family intervention for schizophrenia. *The Cochrane Library (Issue 1)*.

Rachman, S. (1993). Obsessions, responsibility and guilt. *Behaviour Research and Therapy, 31*(2), 149–154.

Rachman, S. (1997). A cognitive theory of obsessions. *Behavior Research and Therapy*, 35(9), 793–802.

Rachman, S. J. & De Silva, P. (1978). Abnormal and normal obsessions. *Behavioural Research and Therapy, 16*, 233–248.

Read, J., Perry, B. D., Moskowitz, A. & Connolly, J. (2001). The contribution of early traumatic events to schizophrenia in some patients: a traumagenic neurodevelopmental model. *Psychiatry, 64*(4), 319–345.

Rector, N. A. & Beck, A. T. (2001). Cognitive behavioural therapy for schizophrenia: an empirical review. *Journal of Nervous and Mental Disease, 189*(5), 278–287.

Romme, M. A. & Escher, A. D. (1989). Hearing voices. *Schizophrenia Bulletin, 15*, 209–216.

Salkovskis, P. M. (1985). Obsessional-compulsive problems: a cognitive behavioural analysis. *Behaviour Research and Therapy, 23*, 571–583.

Salkovskis, P. M. (1991). The importance of behaviour in the maintenance of anxiety and panic: a cognitive account. *Behavioural Psychotherapy, 19*, 6–19.

Salkovskis, P. M. (1996). The cognitive approach to anxiety: threat beliefs, safety-seeking behaviour, and the special case of health anxiety and obsessions. In P. M. Salkovskis (ed.), *Frontiers of Cognitive Therapy*. New York: Guilford Press.

Salkovskis, P. M. & Kirk, J. (1989). Obsessional disorders. In K. Hawton, P. M. Salkovskis, J. Kirk & D. M. Clark (eds), *Cognitive Behaviour Therapy for Psychiatric Problems: A Practical Guide*. Oxford: Oxford Medical Publications, Oxford University Press.

Salkovskis, P. M., Forrester, E., Richards, H. C. & Morrison, N. (1998). The devil is in the detail: conceptualising and treating obsessional problems. In N. Tarrier, A. Wells & G. Haddock (eds), *Treating Complex Cases: A Cognitive Behavioural Therapy Approach*. Chichester: John Wiley & Sons.

Sensky, T., Turkington, D., Kingdon, D. et al. (2000). A randomized controlled trial of cognitive-behavioural therapy for persistent symptoms in schizophrenia resistant to medication. *Archives of General Psychiatry, 57*(2), 165–172.

Sham, P. C., Jones, P., Russell, A. et al. (1994). Age at onset, sex, and familial psychiatric morbidity in schizophrenia. Camberwell collaborative psychosis study. *British Journal of Psychiatry, 165*, 466–473.

Skeate, A., Jackson, C., Birchwood, M. & Jones, C. (2002). Duration of untreated psychosis and pathways to care in first-episode psychosis: investigation of help-seeking behaviour in primary care. *British Journal of Psychiatry (supplement), 43*, S73–S77.

Stirling, J., Tantum, D., Thonks, P., Newby, D. & Montague, L. (1991). Expressed emotion and early onset schizophrenia. *Psychological Medicine, 21*, 669–672.

Strauss, J. S. (1969). Hallucinations and delusions as points on continua functions. *Archives of General Psychiatry, 21*, 581–586.

Sullivan, H. S. (1927). The onset of schizophrenia. Reprinted in the *American Journal of Psychiatry, 151*(6), June 1994, Sesquicentennial Supplement 135–139.

Tarrier, N., Barrowclough, C., Porceddu, K. & Fitzpatrick, E. (1994). The Salford family intervention project: relapse of schizophrenia after 5 and 8 years. *British Journal of Psychiatry, 165*, 829–832.

Tarrier, N., Yusupoff, L., Kinney, C. et al. (1998). Randomised controlled trial of intensive cognitive behaviour therapy for patients with chronic schizophrenia. *British Medical Journal, 317*, 303–307.

Tien, A. (1991). Distributions of hallucinations in the population. *Social Psychiatry and Psychiatric Epidemiology, 26*, 287–292.

van Os, J., Hanssen, M., Bijl, R. V. & Ravelli, A. (2000). Strauss (1969) revisited: a psychosis continuum in the normal population? *Schizophrenia Research, 45*, 11–20.

Verdoux, H., Maurice-Tison, S., Gay, B. et al. (1998). A survey of delusional ideation in primary care patients. *Psychological Medicine, 28*, 127–134.

Warner, R. (2002). Limitations of the Bonn Scale for the assessment of basic symptoms as a screening measure: letter to the editor. *Archives of General Psychiatry, 59*, 5.

Watts, F. N., Powell, G. E. & Austin, S. V. (1973). The modification of abnormal beliefs. *Behaviour Journal Medicine and Psychology, 46*, 359–363.

Wegner, D. M. (1994). *White Bears and Other Unwanted Thoughts: Suppression, Obsession and the Psychology of Mental Control.* London: Guilford Press.

Wegner, D. M., Schneider, D. J., Carter, S. R. & White, T. L. (1987). Paradoxical effects of thought suppression. *Journal of Personality and Social Psychology, 52*(1), 5–13.

Wells, A. (1995). Meta-cognition and worry: a cognitive model of generalised anxiety disorder. *Behavioural and Cognitive Psychotherapy, 23*, 301–320.

Wells, A. (1997). *Cognitive Therapy for Anxiety Disorders.* Chichester: John Wiley & Sons.

Wells, A. (2000). *Emotional Disorders and Metacognition: Innovative Cognitive Therapy*: New York, NY: John Wiley & Sons.

Wells, A. & Mathews, G. (1994). *Attention and Emotion: A Clinical Perspective.* Hillside, NJ: Laurence Erlbaum Associates.

Wells, A., Clark, D. M., Salkovskis, P. et al. (1995). Social phobia: the role of in-situation safety behaviours in maintaining anxiety and negative beliefs. *Behaviour Therapy, 26*, 153–162.

Yung, A., McGorry, P. D., McFarlane, C. A. et al. (1996). Monitoring and care of young people at incipient risk of psychosis. *Schizophrenia Bulletin, 22*(2), 283–303.

Yung, A., Phillips, L. J., McGorry, P. D. et al. (1998). A step towards indicated prevention of schizophrenia. *British Journal of Psychiatry, 172 (supplement 33)*, 14–20.

Yung, A., Phillips, L., McGorry, P. et al. (2000). *Comprehensive Assessment of At-Risk Mental States (CAARMS).* Full Version 2001 (see below). Unpublished manuscript. University of Melbourne, Australia: The PACE Clinic.

Yung, A., Phillips, L., McGorry, P. et al. (2001). *Comprehensive Assessment of At-Risk Mental States (CAARMS).* Full Version September 2001. Department of Psychiatry, University of Melbourne, Australia: The PACE Clinic.

Zimmerman, M., Coryell, W., Corenthal, C. & Wilson, S. (1986). Dysfunctional attitudes and attribution style in healthy controls and patients with schizophrenia, psychotic depression, and nonpsychotic depression. *Journal of Abnormal Psychology, 95*, 403–405.

Zubin, J. & Spring, B. (1977). Vulnerability: a new view of schizophrenia. *Journal of Abnormal Psychology, 86*, 103–126.

INDEX

activity scheduling 84–5
admissions, trauma of 4–5
age of onset for schizophrenia 12
alcohol use 6
angry thought 48
anxiety, CBT in 29
assessment 47–50
attentional factors 48
attenuated psychotic symptoms 13
attenuated symptoms group rationale 130
auditory hallucinations 51, 60, 88, 89, 91
avoidance 46, 48

basic symptoms, idea of 13
Beck Hopelessness Scale 50
befriending 102
behavioural reattribution methods 51
beliefs
    advantages/disadvantages of 58
    assessment 49–50
    compensatory 95
    declarative 45, 46
    negative 89–90
    positive 87–9
    procedural 45, 46
    see also core beliefs
bereavement 57
Bonn Scale for the Assessment of Basic Symptoms (BSABS) 10, 13–14
Brief Limited Intermittent Psychotic Symptoms (BLIPS) 13, 14–15, 29, 106, 120, 129
Brief Psychiatric Rating Scale (BPRS) 10
bullying 58

catastrophic predictions 66
childhood trauma 118
client-friendly formulation 123

cognitive model
    CT based on 31
    describing onset of psychosis 45–7
cognitive therapy 26, 66
    education 34
    form of 30
    group-based interventions 30
    guided discovery 34
    future use in psychosis 119
    homework 34–6
    individual 30–6
    reason for 29–30
    shared problems and goals 32–4
    structure of sessions 31–2
    as time-limited intervention 36
cognitive-attentional syndrome 87
cognitive-behaviour therapy (CBT) 29
cognitive-behavioural therapy 24
collaboration 40–1
Community Mental Health teams (CMHTs) 62
compensatory beliefs 95
Comprehensive Assessment of At-Risk Mental States (CAARMS) 10, 13
confidants, lack of 105
coping with onset 6
core beliefs
    case example 96–9
    identification 93–4
    modification of 94–6
costs of detection 6
critical period, concept of 7
criticism, fear of 99

decatastrophising symptoms 62
declarative belief 45, 46
delusions 45
Department of Health: Early Intervention Policy Implementation Guide (2001) 12

depression 5, 46, 84
  CBT in 29
downward arrow technique 93–4
dreams diary 90
drug use 6, 88
  assessment 50
Duration of Untreated Illness (DUI) 6
Duration of Untreated Psychosis (DUP)
    3–4, 26
dysfunctional thought control 46
dysfunctional thought records (DTRs) 35,
    94
dysthymia 29

*Early Intervention Policy Implementation
    Guide* (2001) (DoH) 12
Early Psychosis Prevention and Intervention
    Centre (EPPIC) 11
EDIT team (Birmingham) 17
EDDIE study 19, 20–1
engagement
  case example 39–40
  difficulties in 41–2
  principles of 37–9
European Predication of Schizophrenia
    (EPOS) study 14
evil, feelings of being 99
experiment sheet 127
expressed emotion (EE) 103

family group rationale 131
family interventions 30
formulation-driven interventions 31,
    51–2

gender, age of onset for schizophrenia 12
General Health Questionnaire (GHQ) 15
generalised anxiety disorder 87
generating alternatives form 83, 125
genetic predisposition 9
Global Assessment of Functioning (GAF)
    13
GP, relationship with 38
guided discovery 34, 40, 69
guilt, feelings of 99

hallucinations 45, 60, 88, 89, 91
helplessness 99
historical factors 49
homelessness 42
homework 108–9
  CT and 34–6

Huber, Gerd 13
hypervigilance 106

identification
  of cases 16–21
  process of 15–16
  of psychosis, primary care guidelines
      133
idiosyncratic formation 51–3, 97, 108
  interpretation of intrusions in catastrophic
      manner 71
  interpretation of intrusions using
      normalising information 72
imagery 65–6
incidence of psychotic phenomena 57
indicated prevention approach 24
Interpretations of Voices Inventory 91
intervention, choice of 24–6
interviews, conducting 47–9
intrusions 48, 65–8
  case studies 68–71
  questions in evaluation 71–4
isolation 5
  therapy and 105

Kraepelinian concept of psychosis 7, 59,
    117

language, use of 38

major depressive disorder 29
McGlashan, Thomas 14
McGorry, Patrick 11
measures
  for defining risk 9–10
  general 10
  specific to at-risk populations 11
media images of schizophrenia 59
Mental Health Act 4
metacognition 29, 45, 48, 87–92
  assessments 90–1
  treatment implications 91–2
Meta-Cognitions Questionnaire (MCQ)
    90–1
meta-worry 89
Morrison's model of psychosis 45, 46
  client-friendly 52
  idiosyncratic 51–3

Needs Based Interventions (NBI) 24–5
negative automatic thought 48
negative beliefs 89–90

neuroleptic malignant syndrome 25
non-attendance 41
normalisation
    case example 60–2
    of information as education 62–4
    need for 57–8
Northwick Park Study 4

OASIS team (London) 17
obsessions 46
obsessive-compulsive disorder 87
olanzapine 25
onset of psychotic illness 5
ORYGEN Youth Health Service 11

panic 46
panic attacks 79, 118
panic disorder 51
paranoia 5, 38, 88
paranoid thought 48
parent–child relationship 5
peripheral questioning 79
persecutory delusions 89
Personal Assessment and Crisis Evaluation
        (PACE) 11–12, 13, 24, 119
Phillips, Lisa 11
Positive and Negative Syndrome Scale
        (PANSS) 10, 14, 15, 16, 21
positive beliefs 87–9
post-traumatic stress disorder 5, 118
pre-psychotic population 26
pre-schizophrenic population 26
prevalence of psychosis 9
prevention strategies 23–4
    indicated 24
    selective 24
    universal 23–4
problem lists 32–3, 107
problem-orientated interventions 32–3
procedural beliefs 45, 46
prodromal population 26
prodrome 7
    characterisation 111–12
psychoeducation 30

recovery style 112
referrals
    potential sources 16–17, 19
    process 19–20
    rates 19–20
rejection, fears of 99
relationships, loss of 5–6

relapse in psychosis 58
relapse prevention 111–20
    practical application 112–13
    reason for 111–12
    therapeutic blueprint 113–14
risk assessment 50
risk factors for psychosis 11–12
risk, measures for defining 9–10
risperidone 24

safety behaviours 46, 47, 48, 60, 75–85
    activity scheduling 84–5
    assessment 75
    case example 77–80, 82–4
    examples 76
    experimenting 76–7
    selective attention as 81–2
    testing of 35–6
schizophrenia
    client's message 59–60
    clinician's message 59
    Kraepelinian view of 59
    prevalence 9
schizotypal personality disorder 13
scoring guidelines for identification of
        at-risk groups 15
selective attention 46
    as safety behaviour 81–2
selective prevention approach 24
self-blame 88
self-harm 60
self-regulatory executive function (S-REF)
        model of emotional disorders 45, 81, 87
self-schemas 29
service setting 41
side-effects of antipsychotic medication 25
SMART 33, 36, 107
social anxiety 5
social isolation 101–9
social phobia 46, 98, 95
social support, accessing 101–5
    loss of 103–4
sociocultural background 38
Socratic approach 77
Socratic dialogue 34, 66, 71, 74
state factors 13
stigma 5, 26
    CT and 29–30
stress–vulnerability models 12–13
Structured Interview for Prodromal
        Symptoms and Scale of Prodromal
        Symptoms (SIPS/SOPS) 10, 14, 25

suicidal thoughts 50, 79
suicide 5

thought–action fusion 63, 90
thought–emotion–behaviour cycles 53
thought suppression 63
timing of engagement 41
training in CT 118–19
trait factors 12–13
transition rates 20–1, 24–5

universal prevention approach 23–4

venue for therapy sessions 40–1
verbal hallucinations 57, 60, 88, 89
verbal reattribution methods 51

weekly activity sheet 128
worthlessness, feelings of 49–50, 99

Yung, Alison 11, 14, 24